Helping
Ourselves

Other Norton/Worldwatch Books

Lester R. Brown
*The Twenty-Ninth Day: Accommodating Human Needs
and Numbers to the Earth's Resources*

Lester R. Brown, Christopher Flavin, and Colin Norman
*Running on Empty: The Future of the Automobile
in an Oil Short World*

Erik P. Eckholm
Losing Ground: Environmental Stress and World Food Prospects

Erik P. Eckholm
The Picture of Health: Environmental Sources of Disease

Denis Hayes
Rays of Hope: The Transition to a Post-Petroleum World

Kathleen Newland
The Sisterhood of Man

Helping Ourselves

Local Solutions to Global Problems

Bruce Stokes

A Worldwatch Institute Book

W. W. Norton & Company
New York London

Library of Congress Cataloging in Publication Data
Stokes, Bruce.
  Helping ourselves.
  "A Worldwatch Institute book."
  Includes bibliographical references and index.
  1. Social problems.   2. Social participation.
  3. Self-help groups.   I. Title.
HN18.S856   362'042   80–27042

ISBN 0–393–01362–6
ISBN 0–393–00054–0 pbk.

W.W. Norton & Company, Inc. 500 Fith Avenue, New York, N.Y. 10110
W.W. Norton & Company Ltd. 25 New Street Square, London EC4A 3NT

1 2 3 4 5 6 7 8 9 0

To Wendy

Contents

Acknowledgments

An author's intellectual debts are many and it is impossible to fully acknowledge the inspiration for a complex set of ideas. But I would like to pay special tribute to Carroll Quigley of the School of Foreign Service of Georgetown University who taught me that the traditional conservative virtues of individual initiative and strong community organizations can form the basis of a progressive movement to empower people at the local level.

The analysis of the actual and potential contribution of self-help efforts to global problem-solving has long been relegated to the dustbin of economic studies. I wish to thank Lester R. Brown, president of Worldwatch Institute, for his unflagging interest in and support of my efforts to shed some light on this topic and for his willingness to expand the scope of work at Worldwatch Institute to include this subject. Without the intellectual and financial resources of Worldwatch Institute this book could not have been written.

I am grateful to all those friends and colleagues who took time out of their busy schedules to review early drafts of *Helping Ourselves*. Their comments and criticisms enriched the analysis immensely. The entire manuscript was reviewed by: Alan Berg, George Brockway, Lester Brown, Christopher Flavin, Robert Fuller, Jerry Hagstrom, Arthur Naparstek, Denis Hayes, Kathleen Newland, Colin Norman, Frank Riessman, Lawrence Susskind, Pamela Shaw, Wendy Sherman, and Linda Starke. I would also like to thank the following individuals who reviewed chapters that dealt with their particular area of expertise: Judith Abramson, Rick Carlson, Erik Eckholm, Judi Loomis, Lester Tepley, John Turner, Paul Sommers, and Lisa Walker.

The seeds for this book were first sown in 1971 when I helped to organize Public Interest Research Groups in a number of states. Working with Kathy Kadane, Ralph Nader, and Donald Ross convinced me that citizen empowerment is worth struggling for. More recently, I have received intellectual and emotional encouragement for this project from many friends, including: Alan Berg, Nancy Dunn, Steve Hellinger, Deaver Kehne, Catherine Lerza, and Bob Mashek. The Webster House Six—Arthur Buchanan, Debra Levin, Rich Liroff, Diane Melish, Michael Rauh, and Martin Shulman—helped put these ideas and ideals to the test in our fight against a condominium conversion. All our lives were enriched in the process.

I would like to extend my thanks to Thomas Reese in Indonesia; Ed Duckles, Eric Holt, and Kaki Rusmore in Mexico; Santiago Roca and Rene Rodriguez Heredia in Peru; and Sergio Fernandez A. in Chile for their assistance during the time that I spent in those countries doing research for *Helping Ourselves*.

I am particularly indebted to Oretta Tarkhani who typed the manuscript countless times and whose thoughtful questions helped me to clarify many points. Her diligence in tracking down obscure books and articles was of invaluable assistance to my research. I am also grateful to Blondeen Gravely and Elizabeth Arnault who helped out with the heavy typing load. Christopher Flavin and Pamela Shaw provided timely research support and Macinda Byrd cheerfully protected me from distractions when I needed time to write.

Most authors feel blessed if they have one good editor, I was fortunate to have two. Alia Johnson's able assistance is evident in every chapter of the book. Our long talks helped me to focus my ideas and encouraged me to expand the scope of the book. Anne Norman stepped in on short notice and edited the final chapters with skill and grace.

All authors place special strains on their friendships. Richard Henshaw, a fellow author, was always there when I needed someone to talk to. Moreover, he compiled the footnotes with an attention to detail that is the mark of a true professional.

I am deeply appreciative of the support that Wendy Sherman has given me throughout the writing of *Helping Ourselves*. Her love, her political and intellectual inspiration, and her friendship are more than one should expect from a wife who has a book for a rival.

BRUCE STOKES
August 1980

*Worldwatch Institute
1776 Massachusetts Avenue, N.W.
Washington, D.C. 20036*

1

Introduction

People have lost control over many of the issues that affect their daily lives. The price of energy is set by foreign governments. The economic futures of small towns are often decided in distant corporate boardrooms as a byproduct of company planning. The quality and the nature of social services are determined by impersonal bureaucrats.

Individuals and communities have come to rely on governments, corporations, and professional elites to do many of the things that they once did for themselves. Societies have turned to highly centralized, technologically sophisticated methods of coping with rising energy prices, housing and food shortages, a burgeoning population, and other major problems. We have forgotten that human problems require solutions on a human scale.

Many of the issues that will dominate public concern over the next few decades—energy, food, health care, housing, population, industrial productivity, and the quality of work life—will only be solved through human action and interaction. These global problems will often best be dealt with by people doing more to help themselves at the local level. For it is at the personal and community level that the consequences of problems are most obvious, the motivation to solve them is most direct, and the benefits from action are most immediate. People can create local solutions to global problems by taking charge of the process of problem solving and by changing their values and behavior in response to today's economic and social conditions. By so doing, they can mold more democratic, self-reliant societies.

This task will not be easy. The power of the state has been expanding for years. In order to manage a diverse economy and to provide necessary social services, the size and the number of government agencies have grown substantially, in rich and poor countries, in socialist and capitalist economies alike. The expansion of the public sector can be gauged by the rise in government spending. In the United States, for example, government expenditures grew from 28 percent of the gross national product (GNP) in 1962 to 32 percent in 1978. In Brazil, they rose from 12 to 35 percent of the GNP during the same period; in France, from 36 to 43 percent; and in Sweden, from 36 to 62 percent.[1]

The role that corporations play in modern life has grown at a similar pace, responding to and helping to create consumer demand for ever increasing production of a widening range of goods. In the name of efficiency and profits, most national economies are now dominated by a handful of corporations. In the United States, two hundred industrial firms account for about 30 percent of all private production, and many major sectors of the economy are controlled by a few companies.[2] In socialist economies, a giant state corporation is generally the sole producer of a particular product. Multinational corporations have further centralized the world economy. Six grain companies control almost all international grain shipments and seven oil companies now account for most of the massive international flow of petroleum.

As government and business have grown, a professional-managerial elite has emerged to staff public and private bureaucracies. The expansion of scientific knowledge and the technical complexity of modern issues have led to a dramatic increase in the number of doctors, lawyers, engineers, psychologists, social workers, and other specialists. As a result, human problems that were once dealt with informally are increasingly the exclusive preserve of experts. Narrowly specialized knowledge has supplanted tradition and common sense as the criterion for everything from designing buildings to educating children.

These trends toward centralization and specialization cannot continue indefinitely. Bureaucratic, technocratic solutions will not work for many of the problems now facing humanity. Large agribusiness enterprises cannot ensure adequate diets for the rapidly growing populations of the Third World; only by producing more of their own food can the poor construct a buffer against malnutrition and rising food prices. The major causes of death and illness in industrial and developing countries will not be eradicated by more doctors; better health requires improvements in income, changes in life-style, and a cleaner environment. Government family-planning experts cannot slow the rate of population growth; smaller families will depend on the childbearing decisions of millions of individual couples.

Moreover, many private and public institutions have grown so large that they are no longer efficient, sensitive mechanisms for solving problems. Having expanded over the years on the premise that bigger is always better, their size now often inhibits their function. In large organizations, as employees spend more time in pointless meetings and on redundant paperwork, they have less time to produce quality products or to serve the public. The hierarchical structure of large bureaucracies can be counterproductive when it insulates bureaucrats and corporate executives from the public's needs and feelings. Experience with relatively small businesses and small government agencies suggests that economies of scale can be achieved in organizations of moderate size, so that institutions need never become little worlds unto themselves.

The cost of solving problems in a centralized manner has also become prohibitively expensive. At the national level, citizens cannot afford the growing tax burden of big government. The average American's taxes rose from 19.4 percent of taxable income in 1975 to a projected 22.7 percent in 1981. Internationally, the price tag of meeting the Third World's most pressing problems is more than double the current amount of foreign aid. The World Bank estimates it would cost at least $47.1 billion a year (in 1975 dollars) to upgrade existing services to meet basic needs for food, water, housing, health, and education between 1980 and 2000; in 1975, foreign aid from all sources totaled only $18.4 billion. The political will to solve problems by further increasing taxes and transferring resources from the rich to the poor does not exist. As a result, less expensive solutions to many problems are necessary.[3]

Finally, the depersonalized values fostered by large institutions and elitist professions have begun to alienate many individuals and communities. Assembly-line workers can become unthinking, irresponsible employees when they are ignored and disparaged. Communities whose cultural and social traditions have been trampled in the name of "progress" can turn inward and become reactionary.

State and corporate dominance of problem solving engenders a sense of dependency and helplessness that undermines people's capacity to be active, informed citizens. As social critic Ivan Illich has observed, "Whether the product is provided by an entrepreneur or an apparatchik, the effective result is the same: citizen impotence."[4] When people lack confidence in their ability to deal with the economic and social issues that confront them, they are easily tempted to turn over even more of their rights and responsibilities to authoritarian political movements and to elites who promise quick solutions to complex issues. To avoid this eventuality, there is a need to reinvigorate citizens' ability to help themselves.

There is already mounting dissatisfaction with the shortcomings and the alien values of the overgrown, expensive institutions that now monopolize problem solving in modern society. In the United States, for example, opinion surveys show that 42 percent of the public had confidence in the leaders of government in the mid-sixties; this figure had fallen to 18 percent by 1979. Public confidence in the leaders of major companies fell from 55 percent to 18 percent during the same period, and confidence in leaders of the medical profession fell from 73 percent to 30 percent.[5]

It is clearly time for a change. Just like a stream that carves a new channel if the old one is blocked, societies need to circumvent existing institutions that have proved ineffective. A new approach to problem solving and a new set of values are needed in this era of energy shortages and stagnating economies. Self-help efforts, in which individuals and communities take greater control over the issues that affect their lives, constitute a more effective way of dealing with many of today's problems. By breaking up issues into their component parts and dealing with them at the local level, interdependent problems can once again become manageable. The self-help movement—in health care, in energy, and in housing—can begin to regenerate society's capacity to deal with its problems and its ability to cope with the unprecedented changes facing humanity in the years ahead.

Through self-help activities, the psychology of dependence can be replaced by a growing sense of self-reliance. If homeowners use solar energy to heat their houses, for example, they will be less at the mercy of oil companies and the petroleum exporting countries. If people take better care of themselves

and practice simple self-care techniques, they will be less dependent on the increasingly costly medical-care system.

Self-help initiatives can create a new sense of community, as
people work together to accomplish things that they could not
achieve alone. The ethic of self-interest that dominates much
of modern social interaction can be moderated by a concern for
collective interests. In industry, worker participation to improve economic efficiency and the quality of work life can lead
to cooperation instead of confrontation between labor and
management. In the villages of the Third World, cooperative
efforts to build homes or to increase food supplies can help
overcome centuries-old class and ethnic barriers.

Like any effort to deal with complex issues, individual and
collective self-help activities will benefit from an organizational
framework. An appropriate one already exists in the formal and
informal social networks—the neighborhood friendships and
voluntary associations—that can be found in all communities.
These are ideal vehicles for self-help efforts, for nearly everyone
is a member of some social network. Local clubs and organizations are small, decentralized units that people can compre-
hend and control. Public policies in support of self-help activities can work through these community networks to foster
change.

Experience with broad-based self-help efforts suggests that
individuals and communities can make a substantial contribution to the well-being of nations. No attempt has ever been
made to estimate the actual or potential economic value of
self-help efforts in the United States, but the total would surely
be significant. Already, half of all housing rehabilitation is done
through self-help and one-tenth of all vegetables are homegrown. In Kenya, by comparison, where such efforts have been
formalized into the national Harambee ("pull-together")
Movement, self-help activities contribute over 30 percent of all
development investment in rural areas.[6] Organized community self-help efforts in other societies could bear similar fruit.

Although people can begin doing more for themselves at the

community level, this does not mean that government agencies, corporations, and the professions will become superfluous. Obviously, many things—from building roads to performing brain surgery—are best dealt with by the state or by people with particular expertise. One of the public policy challenges of the next few decades will be matching self-help activities with appropriate government, business, and professional support. In this manner, a balance can be struck between local solutions to global problems and centralized efforts to deal with the same issues, so that the strengths of each approach can complement one another.

A sense of control over the issues that affect people's daily lives is a topic of growing political importance in the United States and other countries. Conservatives argue that this requires a limit on the role of big government, while liberals attest to the necessity of curtailing big business. But in the past these remedies have often resulted in nothing more than a reshuffling of power between the state and corporations. If individuals and communities are to gain greater control over their lives, then they must do so by empowering themselves.

In any society, political and economic power gravitates to those who solve problems. Over the last few decades, bureaucrats, businessmen, and professionals have accrued power by assuming ever greater responsibility for problem solving. As people take a more active role in solving their problems through self-help efforts, they can begin to take some of that power back into their own hands. No longer powerless, they can begin to create societies that are truly democratic.

2

Worker
Participation

For eight or ten hours a day, while at work, many people have little say over what they do or how they do it. Both the problems of the workplace and the problems of the economy seem beyond their influence. Individuals who take care of a family, make decisions about a home, and plan a future for themselves and their children, leave all this competence and sense of responsibility at the office or plant door. Frustrated and angry, they retrieve them at the end of the day. Employees on the Fiat assembly lines in Turin, in the state bureaucracies in Moscow, or in the post office in New Delhi have little or no control over their daily routine. They are rarely asked for their suggestions on how to improve the products or services they provide or how to make their work more fulfilling.

This lack of worker participation in the management of the workplace is a luxury modern economies cannot afford. In a period of slow gains in productivity and rising employee discontent, the mobilization of the latent energies of workers could create a more efficient and democratic economy. Three factors —new technology, the rising costs of production, and the expectation that work should be humane as well as profitable —are forcing transformations in the workplace. As Michael Maccoby of the Harvard University Project on Technology, Work, and Character points out: "The question is not whether to change work patterns; rather, the question is which kinds of change are going to be accomplished, how, and by whom." General Motors Vice-President George Morris has best answered that question: "Change in the work climate . . . cannot be mandated by management or by the union. . . . The people affected by the change must have a say in determining the nature of the change as well as planning how the change is to be effected."[1]

The Workplace Malaise

There are no easy solutions to the debilitating set of problems facing modern economies. Industries in both rich and poor countries suffer from a slowdown in the growth of productivity. In the seventies, manufacturing productivity in Japan, Sweden, and the United Kingdom—measured as output per hour of labor—grew at less than half of the rate of growth in the sixties. In the United States, an already slow growth rate of 3.0 percent per year slid to 2.2 percent. The productivity of the U.S. economy actually declined in 1979, for only the second time since World War II. In the Soviet Union, the growth rate of agricultural and industrial productivity was nearly halved in the sixties and the early seventies. As Edward Denison, an economist with the Brookings Institution, has observed, "Something important happened to productivity, I don't know what it is, but from the recent experience it is very bad."[2]

Since productivity increases can help offset inflation and create an economic atmosphere that is conducive to new investments and job creation, the recent productivity trends in the industrial world are worrying. The next two decades will see rising prices and possible scarcity of some of the major factors of production, such as energy, raw materials, and land. Traditionally, the infusion of capital, the availability of cheap sources of energy, and the application of new technology have provided the impetuses for rising productivity. But these solutions may prove difficult in the future as competing demands for capital escalate, energy supplies become more costly, and technological breakthroughs become increasingly difficult.

Today's productivity problems are compounded by widespread worker dissatisfaction. A study of U.S. workers by the University of Michigan's Survey Research Center indicated that between 1973 and 1977, "Workers in virtually all occupational and demographic categories evidenced appreciable declines in job satisfaction along with other, quite unmistakable, manifestations of rising discontent." Full-time workers have had an absentee rate of 4.2 percent over the last decade, a figure the Department of Labor believes could be cut in half. Moreover, absenteeism has not declined, despite recent high unemployment rates. In Australia, absenteeism averaged nine and one-half days per worker in 1977, a rate of 4 percent. Worker malaise in the Soviet Union is equally widespread. At the Lenin Komsomol Automobile Plant in Moscow, for example, the annual turnover rate among assembly-line workers was close to 40 percent in 1972.[3]

Disenchantment with work life is, of course, nothing new. "Keeping Saint Monday" (taking the day off) and drinking on the job plagued Josiah Wedgwood's china factories in the eighteenth century. But today the economic cost of such irresponsible behavior is staggering. Matt Witt, in the *International Labor Review*, estimates that if every American worker were absent from work one day less per week, the gross national product would increase by $15 billion. In the Soviet Union, observers estimate that production losses because of drunkenness on the job range between $35 and $40 billion a year.[4]

Managers of modern businesses, who learned their skills in a different era, have few solutions to the problems of worker alienation or the slowing growth rate of productivity. Many union leaders are equally confused. Their narrow focus on better pay and shorter work weeks has failed to compensate workers for the lack of control over their day-to-day work life. The traditional adversary relationship between labor and management only seems to aggravate the situation.

Workers, for their part, have generally accepted the conventional wisdom that economic difficulties like inflation and unemployment are best left to the experts—economists, politicians, business and union leaders. Now, employees are slowly beginning to realize that the problems besetting the economy are their problems. The size of the money supply or the price of oil is beyond a factory worker's control. However, the immediate concerns of individual firms, such as productivity, efficient use of resources, the quality of work life, job stability— all issues that contribute to the health of the economy—are problems that workers *can* help to solve.

A Better Place to Work

Millions of people are trapped in the drudgery of mindnumbing tasks. They have no sense of doing something of value, of performing work that is creative or useful to other people. Frustration arises from the industrial organization of work that breaks down each job into its component parts and then trains people to do each part over and over again. This kind of system, which began with the assembly line, now pervades most offices and much of the service sector. Initially, the material benefits of organizing work in this way blinded people to the human costs. "In the past, the man has been first," wrote Frederick Winslow Taylor, the early twentieth-century father of time-motion studies. "In the future, the system must be first. . . . All possible brain work should be removed from the shop . . . the time during which the man stops to think is part of the time that he is not productive."[5]

This situation must change, however, because the costs of organizing work in a hierarchical fashion, with little regard for the people who do most of the work, are becoming more apparent. Studies by Arthur Kornhauser show a decline in mental health among industrial workers as their control over their work decreases. Sullen employees who hate their jobs are less productive, more unreliable, and often prone to indulge in creative sabotage just to enliven their days. Their work attitudes and habits are not something that can be changed by ever greater discipline or monetary incentives. They can be changed only by a slow and difficult process of personal involvement in decision making, by growing individual responsibility, and, ultimately, by workers adopting fundamentally new attitudes about themselves and their work.

"A workplace isn't a collection of individuals so much as a collection of informal groups," notes Stan Weir in *Rank and File*. "Until you recognize that, you're not really into utilizing the power of the people in the workplace." Thus, collective effort may be one way of bringing about successful change in factories and offices. Group interaction can change an individual's attitudes toward his or her work. A close-knit community in the workplace can build mutual responsibility that may be a more powerful influence to do a good job than any responsibility to the boss. When a worker who once spent the whole day tightening the same bolt over and over again has the opportunity to get involved in other tasks, that person's confidence and sense of worth can improve immeasurably.[6]

This was just what happened in 1972, when the United Auto Workers (UAW), Harman International Industries, and the Harvard Project on Technology, Work, and Character jointly designed a program to cope with employee dissatisfaction at Harman's auto rearview-mirror plant in Bolivar, Tennessee. A preliminary poll showed that more than half the Harman workers thought that their fellow employees sometimes worked badly, slowly, or incorrectly, on purpose. In response, the Bolivar experiment instituted a process of democratic decision-making and evaluation among its 1,000 workers. In a network of shop-floor committees, employees now make decisions about everything from painting walls to redesigning assembly lines.[7]

Harman's experience in Bolivar suggests that a more democratic and cooperative working arrangement allows a company to be more productive and gives workers a more stimulating and equitable environment. Caught up in the new participatory spirit in the plant, one group of women workers decided to sign their products. Assertion of their individual and collective craftsmanship reduced defects and saved the company more than $10,000 a year in previously wasted materials. Social life was affected both inside and outside the factory. The number of women and blacks in the union leadership has increased since 1973 and the union elected a black president for the first time. Employees are free to go home once they have met established quotas, yet many stay on to attend organized classes in everything from guitar playing to advanced mechanics. To build a link with the community, workers opened their classes to the citizens of Bolivar and established a credit union and a child-care center.

Efforts to involve people more directly in their work are often not as successful as the Harman experiment because such initiatives strike at the heart of organizational structures. Human beings are asked to relate to each other differently. Hierarchies flatten out, and decisions are made cooperatively. Power in the organization is redistributed, a process always fraught with difficulties. Despite some of the obvious economic and psychological advantages, quality-of-work-life experiments often fail because the people involved—managers and workers alike—feel threatened by the new relationships that are expected of them. Furthermore, while the changes may be couched in rhetoric about a new management style, workers and unions often fear that the initiatives are really a ruse to get more work from the same number of people for the same pay, and, eventually, to undermine and replace unions. The number of humanization programs at nonunion companies only confirms their fears. Experience indicates that unless workers help design and implement quality-of-work-life experiments, employees have little incentive to change their attitudes, work habits, and ways of relating to each other. Moreover, if workers do not have control over the process, it will be difficult to tap the cooperative energies and social cohesion that can make an enterprise work humanely and efficiently.

A Voice in Decisions

Quality-of-work-life experiments deal largely with the individual worker's environment. They have little to do with the overall internal management of the firm and do not touch on the relationship between the company and the rest of society. If employees do not have some input into management planning decisions, their collective interests can be overwhelmed by events beyond the shop floor. Furthermore, rising expectations are associated with any experiment in the workplace. Once workers have a greater say in the organization of their jobs and a greater sense of their own competence, many will want to continue to expand that influence and control.

Employee self-help in the workplace must eventually include extending the collective bargaining process, creating "works councils" at the plant level, and gaining employee seats on corporate boards of directors. Each of these collective efforts takes place through a social network—a union or a works council—that enables individual workers to exert some influence on the production process.

Sweden has already taken a step in this direction. In 1977, under pressure from the Swedish Trade Union Conference, the government expanded union rights, granting a basic measure of influence in fields not covered by previous contracts. Unions are now guaranteed negotiations on a whole range of management decisions, including personnel decisions and the appointment of foremen. Employers must initiate discussions with unions before they decide on important changes in the workplace—such as switching to a new line of business, reorganizing production methods, or selling the firm. Unions have the right to request negotiations on any other issue. To ensure that such negotiations are not used merely to block owners' actions, the company is free to implement decisions once discussions with workers have been completed.[8]

In other parts of Europe, similar efforts are being implemented to protect the broader interests of the employees and the firm through cooperation rather than confrontation. Labor-management councils now exist in almost every European country. In Germany, all plants and offices with more than five workers have a works council; its duties include negotiating with management over work hours, health and safety issues, plant closings, and layoffs—some of the same functions performed by American union locals but over which German and other European workers traditionally have had little say. The Volkswagen works councils have gone one step further and now have the right to approve the speed of the assembly lines —a revolutionary development.[9]

In Japan, consultative committees exist in over two-thirds of the larger enterprises. Joint decision-making is required only on health and safety questions, but other issues such as large-scale layoffs, transfers, and discipline are first discussed in the committees, with collective bargaining available as a backup measure. In other industrial countries, quality control is done by management inspectors, a policy that is soundly disliked by most workers, who resent someone looking over their shoulders. Assuming that employees can be responsible for their own work, Japanese industries have created nearly 600,000 quality-control groups, each comprised of about ten workers and a foreman. Robert E. Cole of the University of Michigan reports that these groups exert such peer pressure to do a good job that Toyota needs only one inspector for every thirty production workers, compared with a standard ratio of one inspector for every ten workers in American auto plants.[10]

In addition, mid-level managers have greater control over their jobs through the traditional Japanese management system, called *ringi*, which emphasizes consensus decision-making. Many management experts ascribe part of Japan's success in international trade to the fact that Japanese companies spend far more time trying to reach an agreement before putting a proposal into operation than firms in other nations. Usually, a formal consensus is sought among supervisory employees, from the company president down to the shop foreman. Critics say that this process is ridiculously time-consuming, a complaint often made about other forms of democratic governance. But once supervisory personnel at all levels have agreed to a proposal it can be swiftly implemented, with no foot-dragging by disgruntled employees. Japan's economic success suggests that industrial democracy need not be a hindrance to efficiency.

Socialist countries, as well as capitalist ones, are experimenting with increased worker participation. In Yugoslavia, each factory, store, and office has a workers' council. Its wide-ranging powers include economic planning and the right to select the management board, to set wages, and to handle disciplinary problems.[11] A common criticism of self-management is that if everyone has to decide on everything, nothing will get done. The Yugoslav experience, however, indicates that worker participation is most active around decisions on issues of personal relevance, such as wages and working conditions. Employees are content to leave to managers the decisions on the firm's relationship with the outside world, as long as they have some oversight. A democracy is not judged solely by the degree of participation, but by the potential for people to have an impact on decisions that directly affect them. Using this criterion, the Yugoslav system gets high grades.

In the United States, the art of creating shop-floor networks to deal with production and quality-of-work-life problems is still in its infancy. The UAW and the Big Three automakers are conducting employee-participation experiments in several dozen locations. At the General Motors (GM) auto assembly plant in North Tarrytown, New York, for example, small groups of workers and supervisors have broken down the traditionally rigid hierarchy and have cooperated to solve problems. By lowering the accident, absenteeism, and grievance rates and improving the quality of the cars produced, they are generally credited with convincing GM to keep the plant open at a time when it was closing other production facilities. GM now holds the Tarrytown plant in such esteem that it chose Tarrytown to build the company's "new automobile for the eighties."[12]

Works councils and quality-control groups are structures that parallel and complement the traditional management and union organization of the workplace. They create a new community of interest within the factory or office that cuts across the old divisions of responsibility and authority. These new social networks can become vehicles for change in the workplace by creating new levels of employee involvement in the production process.

Many major business decisions are not made on the shop floor or brought up during collective bargaining, however, but in the boardroom. So that workers can have some control over these decisions and thus assume added responsibility for the success or failure of their companies, there is growing interest in placing workers on boards of directors.

The West Germans are pioneers in this respect. Under their system of codetermination, called *Mitbestimmung,* labor and stockholders now have an equal number of seats on the supervisory boards of all major German corporations, including the subsidiaries of such American giants as Ford, IBM, and Proctor and Gamble. Codetermination now reportedly involves nearly 700 German firms with more than 5.6 million workers.[13]

Mitbestimmung was given its greatest test during the economic downturn of the mid-seventies. At Volkswagen, management wanted to cut back the labor force and shift one-third

of production to the United States. Despite evidence from its
own economists that car sales would soon improve, the union
reluctantly agreed to the eventual dismissal of 25,000 workers,
which could ultimately have cost the company as much as $100
million in severance payments. When demand for cars picked
up and the company was forced to rehire laid-off workers,
vindicating the union's original advice, labor representatives on
the board gained new stature. The decision to build Volkswagen Rabbits in the United States was handled with equal
cooperation. The union wrested from management some
concessions on investments to maintain Volkswagen employment in Germany and then bowed to the realities of the market, which dictated shifting production abroad.[14]

Across the Atlantic, formal worker representation on boards
of directors is still anathema to most labor leaders and to
management as well. According to AFL-CIO official Thomas
Donahue, "We do not seek to be a partner in management,
to be most likely the junior partner in success and the senior
partner in failure."[15] Most union leaders see worker participation as a ruse to nullify the historically successful adversary role
of American labor. Management generally agrees that labor
representation on boards would blur the distinction between
the two groups and would be divisive and inefficient.

Yet this tide may be turning. The 1979 UAW contract with
Chrysler included placing union President Douglas Fraser on
the Chrysler board of directors. Both management and the
union realized that worker representatives might help improve
decision making in that financially beleaguered company. It is
increasingly apparent that workers cannot help themselves and
their companies if they only implement decisions. They must
help make them as well.

A Stake in the Business

In any economic system ultimate power rests with those who
control the fruits of production—shareholders, the state, or
employees. Labor-management cooperation on the shop floor

or in the boardroom does not address the issue of who reaps the benefits or bears the burden of the company's economic fortunes. Worker participation divorced from ownership has only a limited potential.

The popular image of worker participation in ownership is collectively run, politically motivated food co-ops or small, alternative businesses. However, workers own a piece of some of the world's better-known enterprises. Sears Roebuck, the largest retail department store in the world with 400,000 employees, is 20 percent worker-owned through a profit-sharing plan.[16]

The University of Michigan's Institute for Social Research estimates that there are more than 1,000 firms in the United States with some small amount of employee ownership (usually by management), not including profit sharing and pension trusts. The U.S. Senate Select Committee on Small Business reports that in at least 90 companies blue-collar employees own a majority interest. Cooperatives, whose popularity seems to go through cycles linked to economic conditions, are again on the upswing around the world. Co-ops now account for nearly 3 percent of the Italian gross national product and employ more than 170,000 workers. Despite a state-controlled economy, Polish workers' co-ops employ 800,000 people and are responsible for one-third of all clothing, one-quarter of all footwear, and one-fifth of all furniture produced in the country.[17]

U.S. workers, through their pension funds, already indirectly control 20 to 25 percent of the equity in American corporations listed on the New York Stock Exchange. There are also more than 3,000 U.S. companies with Employee Stock Ownership Programs (ESOPs). These programs allow companies to borrow capital cheaply in return for slowly turning over stock to their workers.[18]

In most cases, stock owned through ESOPs is nonvoting stock, and pension-fund owned stock is controlled by management or investment counselors. But it will only be a matter of time before workers want direct control over the use of their money. British unions are already demanding a say in the investment of their £38 billion in pension funds, and the AFL-CIO has decided to push for a greater labor voice in the management of their unions' pension reserves.

In one-quarter of the firms in the United States that have some employee ownership and in many of the worker-owned firms in other countries, workers or worker-community groups exert complete control. Many of these ownership situations were born of necessity, when workers faced unemployment if they did not buy their factories. Such action could end up throwing good money after bad if the company involved is in a dying industry. But often factories are closed, not because they are losing money, but because they are not making enough money. Such was the case when Sperry Rand decided in 1976 to liquidate its library-furniture factory in Herkimer, New York, despite the fact that the plant was making a 22 percent return on invested capital. To avert the loss of 270 jobs and a $3 million payroll, the community bought the plant and is slowly selling it off to the workers. Local-level economic self-help redeemed a potentially disastrous situation for a small town. Although not every community may be as successful as Herkimer, local groups can influence their economic destinies.[19]

Depressed business conditions point to more such efforts in the decades ahead. Already, three out of every four U.S. employee-owned companies formed since 1971 have been set up because of divestiture by conglomerates. The most widely publicized of these efforts, one that ultimately failed, involved the Lykes Corporation's decision to close the Campbell plant of Youngstown Sheet and Tube in Ohio. It was at that time the largest nondefense-related plant closing in the United States since World War II, and it had a devastating impact on the local economy.[20]

The community of Youngstown and the local workers argued, "We want jobs, not welfare." Rather than have government aid come to them once they were out of work, they pushed the federal government and the state of Ohio to loan them money to buy and rehabilitate the plant and keep it open. The price tag was a stiff $245 million in loan guarantees. Initially, the government was interested. "What intrigued us," recalled John Simmons, deputy director of the Department of Housing and Urban Development's Office of Policy Planning, "was the potential of Youngstown as an experimental model of self-help—people in the community attempting to help themselves on their own."[21]

The problem was that the Youngstown community could not go it alone. The very size of the project eventually scuttled the idea. Community and employee economic self-help efforts seem to work best when they are small enough for local groups to manage with local resources. Although the Youngstown experiment in worker-community ownership never got off the ground, there are bound to be more towns facing plant closures and thus more opportunities for worker-community intervention.

The threat of rising unemployment has also sparked worker-ownership initiatives in other parts of the world. Anthony Wedgewood Benn, industry secretary in the British Labor government in the mid-seventies, funneled government money to three enterprises—the Meriden Motorcycle Works, the *Scottish Daily News,* and Kirby Manufacturing and Engineering—to keep them operating under worker control. In Italy, between 1974 and 1978, roughly 100 firms faced with liquidation were converted into co-ops, saving nearly 10,000 jobs.[22]

In Chile, economic chaos in the seventies rivaled that of the Depression; many workers were forced into management and ownership roles in order to protect their jobs. When General Augusto Pinochet took power in late 1973, he championed an economic policy of free market competition and attempted to sell off state-owned enterprises, which by that time accounted for over 40 percent of industrial production. The company's workers were often the only interested buyers. Today, more than 5,000 workers own some fifty firms, including the largest toothpaste container factory, one of the country's two wallpaper factories, and its largest woolen textile plant. With no support from the Chilean government, but with substantial injections of start-up capital from overseas aid, the firms are holding their own. Four or five new worker-owned companies in Chile are formed each year.[23]

It would be misleading to say there is a global trend toward economic self-help through worker ownership. The *Scottish Daily News* failed soon after it became worker-owned. The Peruvian government attempted to impose employee ownership on a reluctant work force in the mid-seventies and the experiment failed. For the time being, the limited number of worker-owned firms are laboratories where employees are exploring new responsibilities and testing new forms of decision making.

The era of the worker-capitalist is not at hand, but the worsening world economy will create opportunities for greater worker participation. As companies on the edge of the economy are threatened with failure, the prospect of disrupted local economies and destroyed livelihoods will force people back on their own resources and worker or worker-community ownership will become an attractive alternative. As capital becomes more expensive, companies will turn with increasing frequency to their employees to raise the vast sums needed for production, for pollution-control equipment, or for an infusion of cash just to keep the doors open. The 1979 UAW-Chrysler contract was a harbinger of things to come. In return for deferring benefits worth $450 million, workers received stock in the company—a breakthrough for worker participation in a major U.S. company. The UAW estimates that ultimately its members stand to own about one-sixth of the company's stock.

Worker Participation and Economic Performance

The success of self-help at the plant level can be judged by many criteria. The control people feel over their lives and the satisfaction they derive from their work when they have greater mastery over it are certainly at the top of that list. Such humanistic concerns are the heart and soul of any reform in the workplace. Without these objectives, worker participation is a sham. Unfortunately, there is no way to quantify the impact of worker participation on people's psyches. Questionnaires that ask participants in workplace experiments, "Do you find your work more fulfilling now?" are an inadequate measure of what it means to people to have greater responsibility for what they do every day.

The economic effects of worker participation, however, can be measured. In a world increasingly concerned with economic performance, worker-participation experiments will often be judged by how they influence employee efficiency. The subject is a matter of debate. A 1975 survey, funded by the National Science Foundation, evaluated 57 field studies of worker-participation experiences in the United States and found that 4 out of 5 reported productivity increases. A 1977 study of 103 U.S. worker-productivity experiments by Raymond Katzell of New York University confirmed these findings. Karl Frieden, in a 1980 study for the National Center for Economic Alternatives, concluded that "the scientific rigor of many of the studies on workers' participation is less than ideal. However, a clear pattern emerges . . . supporting the proposition that increases in workers' participation result in improvements in productivity."[24]

The Trilateral Commission's Task Force on Industrial Relations was less enthusiastic on the question, arguing that "there is not very strong evidence that these new methods of organizing work have been conspicuously more successful than the more orthodox authoritarian style of management in achieving industrial efficiency measured in terms of output."[25] Nevertheless, nothing in the literature suggests that participation significantly harms productivity.

In individual firms, the productivity gains from worker participation are impressive. Paul Bernstein of the University of California at Irvine has found that output per hour of work in sixteen employee-owned plywood mills in the American Pacific Northwest is 26 to 43 percent higher than in conventionally owned mills. At Tembec Forest Products, Inc., in Canada, productivity rose by 30 to 40 percent in the first three years after workers bought a share of the business in 1973.[26]

The positive correlation between participation, productivity, and economic performance was confirmed in the study of employee ownership by the University of Michigan's Institute of Social Research. The thirty employee-owned firms included in the survey had higher profits than did conventionally owned firms in the same industry. Further, the Institute found that while minor participation in ownership may not necessarily be associated with higher productivity, in general the more equity owned by workers, the greater the profitability of the company. A similar study of forty-two West German firms with some degree of worker participation, including employee share-holding, found that those companies most committed to worker participation were the most efficient and the most profitable.[27]

A U.S. Senate Finance Committee analysis of almost 100 companies with employee stock-ownership programs indicated that, in the average three-year period covered by the survey, the companies realized a 72 percent increase in sales, a 37 percent increase in employment, and a 157 percent increase in profits.[28] These figures compare favorably with traditionally owned firms.

Whether the benefits of worker participation will continue over time remains to be seen. Certainly, short-term improvements may prove fleeting if workers do not receive some direct economic gain from participatory work changes. The U.S. Department of Health, Education, and Welfare's *Work in America* warns that "the redesign of work tasks through participation will increase productivity, but some experience has indicated that without profit sharing, workers may feel that they have been manipulated and productivity may slip back to former levels."[29] More broadly speaking, there will be no economic benefits from worker participation if workplace democracy is mere window dressing. If employees are going to participate, then power and the fruits of economic success must be democratically apportioned.

Laying the Groundwork for Participation

Examples of economic self-help indicate that there is an untapped reserve of human energies and commitment in industrial economies. The management and ownership patterns that have evolved from the entrepreneurs of the nineteenth century to the conglomerate and state industry bureaucracies of today are unable to take full advantage of this potential. Authoritarian management was able to generate a surplus in an economic system characterized by abundance. Now, however, faced with slowing economic growth and rising energy and resource costs, management seems unable to cope with lagging productivity and growing worker disaffection. Experience around the world suggests that broadening the responsibility for decision making and problem solving as well as the involvement of those most affected by economic and workplace problems will be essential for successful economic management at the company level and in the economy at large.

The ultimate success of worker participation may rest on the evolution of a new set of workplace values. As writer Daniel Zwerdling points out, "Workers who have been taught for a lifetime to perform isolated tasks, taking orders from a boss, must learn to acquire the confidence, responsibility, and autonomy to make decisions on their own . . . [they] must learn new democratic skills—trivial sounding but crucial skills such as running efficient meetings, analyzing problems, and making decisions effectively in groups."[30]

Changes in employee values are not likely to occur without changes in the attitudes of management. Managers in socialist and capitalist enterprises alike have been taught to value product over process, speed over deliberateness, and decisiveness over consensus. Successful managers of the future will be enterprising, nonauthoritarian leaders who can mobilize human skills, not just technical know-how, to solve problems. Management that can capitalize on the strengths of worker participation will be at a distinct competitive advantage. Umberto Agnelli, managing director of Italy's giant Fiat company, believes that "management must be refined, through careful planning, with the full involvement and participation of all segments of society, including unions. There must be a new decentralizing process of consultation and decision making."[31]

Unions have a special role to play as part of the network of workplace groups involved in worker participation. They have the power to make management listen to workers' ideas. Unions can bring a level of expertise to decision making that has been sorely lacking in many companies. They have the resources—trained leaders, organizational discipline, technical personnel, and money—not available to small firms or unorganized groups of workers. They have credibility with workers that can help in shaping new workplace values. And unions have a vested interest in long-term sustainable management decisions that might be a useful antidote to short-range profit-maximization planning.

Some unions have begun to accept these challenges. Northern European unions have been in the forefront of worker participation experiments. In the United States, a survey by the Bureau of National Affairs shows that there has been a substantial increase in the number of contracts in which unions have pledged to cooperate with management on certain issues.[32]

A political climate supporting worker participation is often a prerequisite for cooperative self-help by workers and management. The European experience suggests that government support may be necessary to obtain effective worker participation, in light of the opposition of most management. The German government has sponsored extensive work humanization experiments, for example. Beginning with a subsidy of $4.3 million in 1974, the government spent more than $40 million on such programs in 1978.[33] Even a modest improvement in productivity or a decrease in absenteeism in a few factories more than justifies this expense.

Lack of start-up capital is often a stumbling block for worker participation in ownership. Governments may need to lend worker enterprises substantial sums of money. Experience indicates that such loans are not the beginning of an endless infusion of government funds forestalling the inevitable demise of a company, but rather are public investments in job preservation and in the revitalization of local economies. The government may be the only institution with the financial resources and the requisite broad social mandate to properly support workers' attempts to buy businesses. The creation of the U.S. National Consumer Cooperative Bank, which can lend up to 10 percent of its funds to production co-ops, is a sign of growing government interest in such ventures.

Government assistance, however, will never be sufficient to meet the expected need. The economic, human, and institutional resources that are necessary to make worker participation effective must come largely from employees themselves and from their immediate communities. In many cases, workers and communities can be partners in ownership, thus sharing the financial burden and ensuring cooperation between workers and the rest of the community.

Worker participation is not, however, a universal panacea for problems of the workplace. Neither the restructuring of the assembly line nor the introduction of teamwork will necessarily improve inherently dirty and tedious jobs. The only way to improve such conditions is to shorten working hours or turn these jobs over to machines.

Also, worker participation is irrelevant to the solution of many economic problems. Although participatory work settings are often labor-intensive, the problem of finding employment for the millions of new job seekers entering the labor markets in developing countries must be resolved by broader social and economic reform. Worker-management cooperation can help firms struggling against technological obsolescence, but it cannot resolve society's dilemma of how to assess the social and economic impact of technological innovation. Worker participation can help direct corporate investment toward the development and production of socially beneficial products, but in the immediate future the market will be the final arbiter in deciding whether new technologies are developed. Matching up available resources—be they human or technological—to get maximum production is a management challenge that workers can contribute to solving. But on a finite planet, the limits to economic growth are beyond workers' control.

Despite these limitations, the higher productivity, improved labor-management relations, and the better work life associated with worker participation argue strongly for new forms of management and ownership. This is increasingly acknowledged. In 1975, two out of three Americans said they would prefer to work for an employee-owned and -controlled company if they were given the choice, and in 1978, nearly half the public said they thought workers should have a greater say in running the companies they work for. Nearly one-third of those surveyed in a 1974 opinion poll in France said the single most important reform they wanted was democratization of the company. Even more important, this sentiment is also growing in the workplace. "Workers have always been told not to get involved, that someone will take care of them," says Ed Mann, president of the steelworkers local in Youngstown. "Well, now we see that if we want something, we have to do it ourselves."[34]

While public and worker opinion may shift with the economic currents, the participatory structures now being built into Western economies, and to some extent into those of other societies, will be around for a long time. Since accountability for one's actions does not end at the plant gate, increased responsibility in the workplace could lead to greater social responsibility outside the workplace on the part of workers and corporations. As people gain more control over issues at work, they will want greater control over other aspects of their lives. In this way, worker participation may be a logical adjunct to neighborhood and individual self-help measures.

3

The Consumer
Energy Resource

The energy crisis has exposed the vulnerability of life in modern societies. Rising energy prices and energy shortages are undermining the world's economic growth and robbing individuals and communities of control over their destinies. Widespread dependence on Middle East oil supplies jeopardizes world peace.

There are no simple solutions to these energy problems. World petroleum production is expected to peak in the next decade, further driving up prices. Coal is not a viable alternative despite vast remaining reserves, because its burning pollutes the air and its mining ruins the land. Moreover, few poor countries have coal reserves. The rising costs of commercial nuclear reactors, problems with nuclear waste disposal, and growing public opposition to plant siting suggest that nuclear power will not become a major source of energy in the near future either.

Faced with these problems, it is little wonder that consumers feel overwhelmed by the energy crisis. OPEC price decisions, dictated by political as much as by economic rationales, are beyond personal control. Energy policy within one's own country seems equally capricious when, for example, communities in New England cannot increase winter supplies of natural gas from Texas and Louisiana.

The frustration and anger that people feel about this situation often obscures the fact that over the next few decades there is little OPEC will do or that the major oil companies can do to solve the energy problem. No more oil is being created under the ground, and no amount of production will be able to keep up with demand if the insatiable hunger for energy continues to increase at the rate of the last few decades.

Consumers, however, are not helpless. The energy future can be determined democratically through energy conservation and reliance on solar energy. As David Lilienthal, former chairman of the Tennessee Valley Authority and the Atomic Energy Commission, has pointed out, "While Congress debates energy policy, while courts and learned experts discuss environmental tradeoffs, while economists pontificate, people in their own communities can do something to help themselves."[1]

The Consumer as Energy Conserver

The energy source consumers can most easily control is, paradoxically, the energy they waste. As energy prices rise, people must begin to realize that many previously innocuous, apparently unrelated decisions in their lives have become decisions about how to use energy. Energy conservation requires no particular expertise and often costs little or nothing. Most people live so far from the thermodynamic boundaries of efficiency that the only immediate constraint on conservation is human ingenuity and the willingness to change habits.

Almost every facet of life in the industrial world is energy inefficient. People go on unnecessary short trips in cars that get poor mileage. Homes are designed to suit the owners' whims rather than external climatic realities. The food people eat is over-refined, over-processed, and over-packaged, and two-ton vehicles are used to transport small quantities of it from supermarket to home. The average person in North America wastes about half the energy that he or she consumes. Since North Americans use one of every three barrels of oil produced in the world, their failure to conserve energy significantly affects global demand for oil and raises the price for everyone else.[2]

The first place people can start conserving energy is in the home. About 20 percent of the energy used in the United States (slightly more in Canada, and a little less in Western Europe and Japan) is used to heat, cool, and light residences and to run appliances. Household energy use can be greatly reduced merely by changing wasteful habits. For example, studies have shown that an American family can use half as much energy as another family living in an identical house, depending on how conscientious it is about energy use.[3]

Policymakers have long neglected the potential for household conservation because, as Robert Socolow of Princeton University points out, "There are no spectacular technical fixes. There is only a catalog of small fixes, many of them drab and unimpressive in isolation. It is therefore easy to dismiss conservation of household energy as an incremental business and to seek solutions elsewhere. But the catalog is fat, and many of its entries are cheap."[4]

Some of the most important "small fixes" an individual can make involve heating the home more efficiently. According to some estimates, two-thirds of American residences need additional thermal insulation, and nearly one-third of British homes are completely without insulation.[5] People can further weatherize their houses by caulking windows and weather-stripping doors. Americans can adopt the European practice of heating only those rooms that are being used instead of the whole house.

Home appliances account for about one-third of all the energy consumed in American households. The major energy user is often the water heater. American families keep thirty to fifty gallons of hot water available day and night, while West German families are satisfied with containers less than half that size, which use correspondingly less energy. Buying a smaller water heater, insulating it, and keeping it at a moderate temperature can reduce energy use without depriving a family of hot showers. People can also save energy by using appliances more efficiently. Preparing food in a pressure cooker saves time and energy in the kitchen. Cooking dinner on the top of the stove uses 30 percent less energy than a microwave oven, which uses approximately 40 percent less energy than a conventional electric stove.[6]

There is already substantial consumer interest in home energy conservation. Between 1975 and 1977, the number of American homes with some insulation increased by one-third. Although other "small fixes" are harder to quantify, such conservation efforts have already had an impact on consumption. American residential energy use, which had been rising by 4.7 percent per year in the sixties, grew at only 2.6 percent in the seventies. Residential and commercial energy use actually declined in the mid-seventies in such countries as Belgium, Denmark, Germany, Japan, and Switzerland.[7] However, the conservation efforts reflected in these trends have barely scratched the surface of energy waste in the home.

How to get from one place to another is often a person's most important daily energy decision, one that has a significant impact on overall energy use. Transportation accounts for an inordinate portion of many countries' energy consumption—about one-third in the United States and one-fifth in the United Kingdom and West Germany. This portion of the energy budget is fat with waste and holds immediate potential for energy savings. Simple car-buying decisions can reduce energy consumption. Good gasoline mileage is already an important consideration for most buyers, and the choice of a standard transmission over an automatic can save one-tenth of fuel use.[8]

Even more important savings will come when people plan their trips wisely, drive less, and walk or bicycle more. For example, a car pool of three commuters who each used to drive to work alone reduces by two-thirds those individuals' gasoline consumption. Using public transit, where it is available, can also mean dramatic energy savings. Walking and cycling substitute food energy, a renewable resource, for petroleum, a nonrenewable resource, as well as providing exercise and a sense of independence that no car driver experiences.

Until recently, skeptics derided the notion that people could change their energy-profligate relationship with the automobile. Now that change has begun. In 1980, for the first time, Americans bought more small cars than gas guzzlers. In the same year there were more than 8,000 van pools in the United States, each taking an average of eight cars off the road. In 1978, public transit ridership in the United States increased by a dramatic 4.5 percent. And bicycle commuting is also on the rise. Sales of bicycles exceeded sales of cars in the United States and West Germany over the last decade, and half of all Japanese families now own a bike.[9] These shifts in commuting habits are still only marginal ones, but they do indicate that new values about personal energy consumption are emerging.

Industry and business are the other major energy users in most advanced societies, and there are opportunities to save energy in each factory and office. Roger Sant, director of the Mellon Institute's Energy Productivity Center, estimates that through better management, industry can reduce energy consumption by 10 to 30 percent, without major capital investment or reduced production. This savings can come largely from what Daniel Yergin of Harvard University calls improved "housekeeping." The best place to start industrial energy housekeeping is on the shop floor. Workers have an intimate understanding of where waste occurs in the production process, so their suggestions can be invaluable to a factory's conservation program. A steel plant official in Ohio described the excellent results his company achieved by working with employees to improve energy efficiency: "A couple of years ago we were having problems with excessive energy use at the open-hearth furnaces. We got the furnace-heater workers together in informal groups and discussed the problems. Within one week, fuel consumption was reduced 20 percent."[10] In many countries industry is the principal user of energy, and major restructuring of industrial processes will ultimately be necessary to use energy most efficiently. But more efficient processes are not required for industry to begin to save substantial amounts of energy; many workers have ideas about how their jobs could be done with greater energy efficiency.

Although the opportunities for individual energy conservation are most apparent in North America, Western Europe, and Japan, energy is also wasted in developing countries. The magnitude of energy waste is much less in these nations because the poor consume less energy to begin with. For them, the question of conservation is not so much cutting back on needless energy use as learning to use energy more efficiently. In the next few years, conservation could prove to be the Third World's most realistic energy option.[11]

In many parts of the Third World, nearly half the energy used is consumed in the home, where there is great potential for savings. Many families cook over open fires or on inefficient stoves, where as much as 90 percent of the heat is lost. Arjun Makhijani, an Indian energy analyst, estimates that, as a result, nearly twice as much energy is used for cooking in the Third World as is normally used by American stoves and ovens.[12] Changing cooking practices and redesigning traditional stoves could reduce firewood consumption by about 40 percent.

In advanced developing countries, like Mexico or India, industry is a major user of energy. Simple "housekeeping" procedures could lead to substantial savings. One Kenyan tire company was able to reduce energy consumption by about one-third, largely by raising the conservation consciousness of its workers. Such efforts in industries throughout the developing world could reduce overall industrial energy use by 5 to 10 percent.[13]

Energy conservation is the first step toward a more secure energy future, both for the individual and for national economies. But the contribution conservation can make to long-term energy security is limited. Once a person has insulated his or her house or begun to take public transit rather than drive to work, that particular self-help activity cannot be repeated. Conservation is not the ultimate answer to the energy problem; it is at best a bridge over current troubled waters. As petroleum supplies dwindle, individuals will have to expand their use of renewable energy resources.

The Consumer as Energy Producer

Like the energy that is conserved, solar energy—from direct sunlight, or captured in the form of falling water, the wind, and organic matter—is a source of abundant power. More energy reaches the earth each day from the sun than all the commercial energy humanity uses from all sources in a year. Worldwide, the energy that could be harvested from green plants each year could provide more power than fossil fuels now annually provide.[14]

Solar energy can permit individuals, communities, and even nations to shape their own energy futures. No one rules the wind or the sun. No company or country can arbitrarily cut off the supply of solar energy or raise its price. The technology used to capture solar energy is diverse and flexible; devices such as solar water heaters and wood-burning stoves enable their users to tap solar energy supplies efficiently and to match their availability with local needs. Solar technology capitalizes on resources that are abundant in many poor countries—sunlight and green plants. Solar devices can often be fashioned from local materials; a few black barrels filled with water on a roof make an adequate solar heater in warm, sunny climates. Solar water and space heaters and some windmills bring out the best qualities of ingenious tinkerers who can adapt them to individual needs.

The easiest way to use solar power is heating with direct sunlight. The Greek playwright Aeschylus wrote that civilized people, unlike barbarians, had houses that "turned toward the sun." It was second nature to our ancestors to design homes with most windows facing toward the equator and with an overhanging roof or shutters to shade windows during the hottest part of the day. When designed so that sunlight falls on an internal brick wall or masonry floor that can store the sun's heat and release it during the night, these simple, passive solar-energy architectural characteristics can save substantial amounts of energy at little or no additional cost.

Active solar heating systems, which trap the sunlight's heat in water or some other material and then use fans to move it about the home, are something each homeowner can use to reduce his or her dependence on insecure and costly energy sources. Even in northern latitudes, such as Canada and Sweden, a good portion of home heating needs could be met by the use of solar collectors. The growing number of homeowners who are pioneering the use of solar energy is evidence that the sun can meet residential energy needs. The Solar Energy Industries Association estimates that there were only 1.3 million square feet of solar panels in the United States in 1974, but by the end of 1979, 48.5 million square feet were in use.[15]

Hot water, a basic necessity for any home, can easily be provided by solar energy. More than two million families in Japan and thirty thousand families in Australia already rely on energy from the sun to heat their water. Four hundred thousand Israeli households—about a third of the country's total—use solar-heated water to bathe and wash dishes.[16] Since a water heater can consume more energy than any other single home appliance, the first task of many homeowners in industrial countries should be to install a solar water heater.

One of the most compelling reasons to begin to rely more on solar energy is the opportunity it provides for families to control their fuel bills. Building a new home with passive solar heating and cooling in mind can cut energy consumption over the life of the building by more than 80 percent. Solar collectors are already cheaper than electrical resistance heating that uses power from a new generating plant, and heating water with sunlight is already cheaper than heating water with natural gas from new wells. The cost of installation is also relatively cheap: all the homes in New Hampshire, for example, could be outfitted with solar water heaters for the price of just one of the much disputed Seabrook nuclear reactors.[17]

Despite these potential savings, the initial high cost of commercial solar technology has meant that, to date, most applications of solar energy have been by middle- and upper-income families. Solar energy should not be a plaything of the well-to-do, but a tool to help all segments of society reduce their dependence on oil and natural gas. There is an unmet need for inexpensive solar collectors that can be adapted for use in the ghettos of industrial countries as well as in the squatter settlements of the Third World.

The transition to an era of greater dependence on renewable energy resources will take time. Consumers experience the vulnerability of dependence on nonrenewable energy resources only indirectly, through price rises and periodic shortages. But the initial capital costs and maintenance problems of solar technologies affect people directly and may dull their enthusiasm, despite the long-term advantages of solar power. Moreover, some solar applications are novel, and people are suspicious of new technologies until they have mastered them. The important thing for consumers is that solar technology is something they *can* master.

Shaping Community Energy Values and Behavior

Individual efforts to conserve energy or to adopt solar technology will make only a small dent in the global energy problem if people act in isolation. Significantly reducing dependence on imported oil supplies will require a concerted effort to change the energy consumption patterns of whole communities. Only through the cumulative effect of millions of individual actions can societies overcome their energy vulnerability.

New energy behavior is not possible without new energy values. It is unrealistic to assume that even the most conscientious person will always turn down the thermostat or invest in new solar technology without a sense of the intrinsic value of those actions. New values must emerge that make it socially irresponsible to buy a gas-guzzling car or to indiscriminately cut down a forest for firewood. Since values are formed within communities, it is within community settings that efforts to develop new energy values must take place. These communities can be as large as an industrial city or as small as an agrarian village. The normal concern of all individuals for what other people think of them can complement self-interest to encourage new behavior.

Davis, California, is one community that has attempted to consciously shape its energy future. In 1968, the citizens elected a progressive city council that launched an effort to create an energy-conservation and solar-energy ethic in the town. Building codes now stipulate the kind and amount of insulation in new housing and encourage architects to design houses to take maximum advantage of passive solar heating and cooling possibilities. A ban on using clotheslines has been lifted so that people can employ solar energy rather than gas or electricity to dry their clothes. A new city ordinance permits people to work out of their homes in order to reduce commuting. Garbage in Davis must be separated to ease recycling, because, according to the head of the waste removal company, "Recycling is important in making the public conscious of its waste . . . through this awareness the public will waste less." Almost every yard has trees to shade houses, thereby cutting the need for air conditioning. Bicycling has become part of the community ethos; the Gay Nineties two-wheeler is the city symbol.[18]

Taken togther, these changes show the effectiveness of tackling the energy problem on a community basis. When one person rides a bicycle to work it is a novelty. When 28,000 of the 36,000 people in Davis own bikes, and bicycles regularly constitute up to 40 percent of the traffic on some main streets, energy self-help efforts take on new significance. Electricity demand in Davis fell by about a fifth between 1973 and 1979, and per capita natural gas use dropped by about a third. Energy conservation and reliance on solar energy have become a way of life in Davis.

Davis is a community with a large university and relatively sophisticated human and institutional infrastructures. Such resources are a valuable aid in devising self-help energy programs, but they are not necessary. The residents of the San Luis Valley in southern Colorado have shown that even the poorest communities can take charge of their energy problems. Firewood has long been the principal fuel for the rural poor in San Luis, but rising costs and scarcities have made it an unreliable energy source. Through a series of community workshops in the late seventies, people became convinced of the merits of solar energy and learned to build simple solar water and space heaters. At least 400 solar systems had been installed by 1980. With more than 3 percent of the Valley's buildings using solar systems, compared with a national average of less than one-half of 1 percent, San Luis may be, on a per capita basis, the solar capital of the United States. Much of this success can be attributed to the way informal social networks spread the word about solar energy. "This is a small community," comments Akira Kawanabe, one of the leaders of the solar energy movement in San Luis. "We know each other by family. . . . Once you get a good thing going, the rumor mill can be one hell of a benefit."[19]

Both formal and informal social networks can provide an

organizational structure for community energy programs that can have an immediate impact on energy consumption. In 1979, in Fitchburg, Massachusetts, for example, schools, community groups, and local businesses banded together to conduct a six-week, city-wide weatherization project. Volunteers trained homeowners in self-help energy conservation techniques. Financial assistance was available for the people who could not afford the materials, and practical help was offered to those who could not undertake the construction themselves. Nearly 3,500 households participated in the program, and each household that completed all the weatherization was expected to lower its fuel bill by as much as 25 percent.[20]

More traditional social networks can also help shape energy values. In 1980, a group of Catholics, Protestants, and Jews formed the Interfaith Coalition on Energy, which plans to use the network of churches and synagogues in the United States to promote a "Covenant of Conservation"—a series of individual and community pledges to conserve energy. It is hoped that by giving energy conservation a major role in educational programs and communal celebrations, some of the capacity of religious institutions to shape values can be used to mold a new energy ethic.[21]

Changing energy values and behavior in the Third World will involve a similar community process. On their own, individuals in Africa, Asia, and Latin America are likely to be no more willing than people in Europe and North America to change habits they enjoy or find convenient. For example, new, more efficient cooking practices are desperately needed to save fuel in many poor areas. Attempts to interest African villagers in solar cookers have frequently failed, however, because they conflict with tradition by requiring midday cooking when the sun is brightest, because they require constant attention when women may need to be doing other things, and because the stoves are often too expensive for the people who need them most.[22] For the individual acting alone, these problems are insurmountable. But if solar cooking technology can be adapted for collective use by existing community groups—an extended family network or the local women's club, for example—many of these cultural and economic obstacles may be overcome. Communal cooking can make noontime meal preparation easier, as families share the labor, and stoves can be cooperatively built to cut costs.

In many parts of the Third World, families are almost completely dependent on firewood for fuel. Individually, it is almost impossible for them to protect woodlots from poachers and to replant depleted forests. But in South Korea this problem is being solved by Village Forestry Associations that have been formed to plant, tend, and harvest woodlots, and to organize the cutting and sale of wood. Watchful neighbors make sure no one abuses the community lot or harvests wood before its time. When wood is cut it is distributed among households, with the profits from the sales of any surplus going into a cooperative fund for other community development projects. By the end of 1977, more than two million acres of woodlots had been established. As one South Korean forestry official has noted: "Village forestry would have failed if the government had simply ordered people to carry it out. Through the associations, villagers have developed a better understanding of their forestry problems and a willingness to work to solve them for their mutual benefit."[23]

Individual Action and National Energy Policy

Since the oil embargo of 1973, many people have assumed that technological innovation will somehow spare them from the necessity of changing the way in which they use energy. Public policy has focused on searching for the key that will unlock the door to a new treasure trove of energy. If technology fails, then rising energy costs are expected to wean society from its wasteful habits and effect a transition to reliance on new energy sources. The role of conscious individual and collective efforts to reduce energy consumption or to increase the use of solar energy has been given short shrift.

People are not pawns in the workings of the technological or economic system. Their intransigence or their voluntary willingness to change their energy consumption habits will play a major role in determining how much and what kind of energy the world consumes in the next few decades.

For example, higher energy prices can change energy consumption habits, but the relationship between price and demand is not the simple one taught by classical economics. In 1974, the year following the first major oil price rise, the average U.S. passenger car was driven less than in 1973, reversing a two-decade trend. But for the next few years, because of inflation, the price of gasoline actually declined relative to the cost of other consumer goods. As a result, gasoline was a good buy, and personal auto travel and the average number of miles driven crept back up to previous levels. Although the 53 percent gasoline price increase in 1979 led to another decrease in driving, the total cost per mile of running a car increased by only about 12 percent.[24] After the initial shock of paying higher gas prices wears off, this small overall price increase suggests that Americans may once again return to their old driving habits. Moreover, if inflation again outpaces gas price rises, the level of energy conservation resulting from higher prices will be much less than expected.

Similarly, the American automobile fleet's gasoline efficiency is expected to improve by 5.2 percent per year through 1990 as a result of more efficient engines and auto design. However, if the average number of miles that each American car is driven begins to increase again at the rate it did from 1974 to 1977, then one-quarter of these yearly gasoline savings will be eaten up by more driving.[25]

If the United States is to reduce oil imports it must cut gasoline consumption, the main source of demand for foreign petroleum. New technologies will help curb consumption and higher prices will induce new consumer behavior. But these are slow, often inequitable, processes. The best way for society to save energy in the short run is through conscientious changes in driving habits and consumer preferences.

In 1979, the United States imported 8.1 million barrels of oil per day. Conservation practices alone could reduce that level of dependence on foreign petroleum by at least 1 million barrels in the short term, without the introduction of new technologies or significant changes in life-styles. The average American home, heated by oil, consumes the equivalent of about 16 barrels of petroleum per year. Simple weatherization could cut that by 2 to 4 barrels per year. If the fifteen million homes now heated by oil were weatherized, oil imports could be cut by 80,000 barrels to 160,000 barrels per day. The U.S. Department of Energy estimates that if all Americans were to lower the average winter temperature in their homes by six degrees, bringing it more in line with temperatures in European homes, then the nation could save the equivalent of half a million barrels of oil per day. Similarly, if all drivers in the United States reduced their personal travel by just ten miles per week, oil imports could be cut by about 300,000 barrels a day. Although not every American is likely to perform all of these self-help activities, if most people engaged in some of them, the resultant energy savings would substantially reduce national energy vulnerability.[26]

The energy savings available from conservation and the use of solar energy in other countries are no less impressive. The non-OPEC developing nations as a group now import about as much oil as the United States. That demand is expected to triple by the end of the century, reaching 20 to 25 million barrels of oil per day. Through efforts to save energy and to shift to other fuels, however, future demand could be as much as one-third lower than it would be otherwise. Greater reliance on solar water heaters, windmills, biogas generating plants, and other solar technologies could reduce oil demand by 1.5 to 4 million barrels per day. Conservation measures could save an additional 2 to 5 million barrels per day.[27]

The value to society of energy conservation and greater

reliance on solar energy is not limited to potential reduction of oil imports. Most self-help energy initiatives that go beyond simple life-style changes create employment. To generate the equivalent amount of energy, the manufacture, marketing, and installation of active solar systems create roughly twice as many jobs as oil or gas production, while weatherization results in ten times as much employment. In the United States, the Department of Labor estimates that energy conservation efforts alone created one million new jobs in 1979, or about one-half of the total employment gain that year. In developing countries, where the level of underemployment is high, the benefit from self-help energy efforts is of particular importance. The Chinese estimate that a biogas generator requires forty to seventy workdays to build, and requires additional labor for maintenance. Although much of this work is not paid employment, it is socially useful, and the payoff comes in cheap and readily available supplies of energy.[28]

Government Supported Energy Self-reliance

Individual and collective efforts to conserve energy and to use solar energy may ultimately prove insignificant, however, without cooperation from government. People cannot ride mass transit that has not been built. City planning and zoning can help cut back on urban sprawl and allow every neighborhood to have a mixture of businesses, stores, restaurants, and movie theaters so that people can walk to shop, to work, or to play. Building codes can require people to construct their homes in a way that uses energy sensibly. And government loans, especially for low-income people, can help overcome the initial financial barriers to energy self-reliance.

The most important thing that governments can do is to provide information and technical expertise at the local level, making it easier for citizens to help themselves. In 1979, in the Anacostia neighborhood of Washington, D.C., public funds were used to train energy auditors who went from door to door assessing energy use and offering expert advice on how to make homes more energy efficient through weatherization and the use of solar water heaters. Because the energy auditors were members of the community, they were readily accepted by their neighbors. In the first year of the program, half the homes in the test area had energy audits, compared with national response rates of only 2 to 3 percent in more impersonal programs run by public utilities.[29]

National treasuries can also invest money in conservation and solar energy rather than spend it on oil imports. In Canada, the government makes grants of up to $425 to people wishing to insulate their homes. Pacific Power and Light Company, a public utility in the northwest United States, decided to give interest-free loans for home insulation when it realized that it cost one-quarter as much to save a kilowatt of power as it did to generate it in a new power plant. The California solar tax credit allows people to write off 55 percent of the cost of buying and installing a solar energy system, up to a maximum of $3,000. California's Energy Commission estimates that the law encouraged the installation of 36,000 solar units between 1976 and 1978, in effect using $22 million in lost tax revenue to encourage people to help themselves.[30]

By funding research into a variety of simple technologies, governments can ensure that consumers have numerous solar options. Buying large quantities of solar hardware for use on public buildings, military installations, and so forth, could create a market that would lower the per-unit cost of solar technologies. As former U.S. Secretary of Energy James R. Schlesinger has argued, "We must make solar energy—like any other energy source—something that can be fitted into the family budget."[31]

Governments have traditionally doled out large subsidies to oil companies and to the builders of nuclear power plants, but they have seldom provided such benefits directly to consumers. Grants, loans, and tax incentives for individuals and communities will be essential to encourage energy conservation and the use of solar energy. Such programs should be generous; every dollar governments invest in conservation will save more energy than would be generated by the equivalent investment in new production capacity. So far, few governments have made this commitment.

Finally, governments can require that citizens conserve energy and use renewable energy resources wherever possible. For example, in parts of northern Australia, where fuels are expensive, solar water heaters are required by law on all new buildings. The same is true of all new public buildings in Israel. San Diego County, California, requires solar water heaters on all new residences, about 4,000 to 8,000 homes a year.[32]

But the passage of a law does not create a new energy ethic. If a law is to work it must reflect community values. Between 1977 and 1979, the people of Portland, Oregon, engaged in a unique effort to shape new laws and new energy values simultaneously. In forty community meetings, the city government sought to build a community consensus regarding energy conservation and solar energy. Finally, a city ordinance was passed to the effect that, after 1985, no building can be sold that is not well insulated. The Portland Planning Commission has been instructed to develop land use policies that encourage high-density development in order to reduce the need for travel. Also, the city government has decided to expand financial incentives for solar energy use and to start a community recycling effort. Through these efforts, Portland hopes to cut energy use by one-third of what it would otherwise be in 1995.[33]

An even more ambitious community effort to shape values and policy began in 1977 in Franklin County, Massachusetts. Citizens in twenty-three of the twenty-six towns in the county formed energy committees. These committees, along with representatives of the utilities, the Cooperative Extension Service, the League of Women Voters, and other community organizations, created the Franklin County Energy Task Force. This group updated a study of the county's energy use, conservation options, and renewable energy resources potential. The task force convinced the county planning board and the county commissioners to approve the first in what is hoped will be a series of five-year energy plans based on their findings. Ultimately, Franklin County hopes to cut energy use by 55 percent and to obtain a substantial portion of its energy from wood, small hydroelectric dams, and other forms of solar energy. The success of this program will depend on the energy network that has been created at the community level in Franklin County. The involvement of local energy committees in the collection and analysis of data, the creation of future energy plans, and the implementation of an energy program will all help citizens change their energy values.[34]

Public authorities can encourage similar community dialogues, energy assessments, and local goal-setting as part of a national policy of energy conservation and greater reliance on solar energy. By using local-level participatory processes to create national energy goals, governments can maximize the contribution individuals and communities can make to the solution of the energy problem. By working closely with churches, neighborhood organizations, and social groups, governments can build a political constituency for energy frugality and the use of renewable energy resources. Moreover, the involvement of communities in energy planning can create lasting social norms that have more power to shape habits than do the marketplace or government rules and regulations. In the spirit of "keeping up with the Joneses," people can be encouraged to adopt solar technologies or to conserve energy long before they might have done so for purely economic reasons.

A national energy strategy made up of individual and community initiatives is a great leap made up of a series of small steps. Through such efforts people can moderate the impact of the energy problem on their lives. As the consumer becomes a conserver and an energy producer, the portion of family expenditure devoted to energy, which in recent years has been on an inflationary spiral, can slow, stabilize, or even begin to decline. As communities become more energy self-reliant, their economies will be less susceptible to disruptions caused by rising fuel prices and gasoline shortages. With local energy self-reliance as the keystone of national energy policy, it will be possible to markedly reduce the vulnerability associated with dependence on imported oil.

4

A Roof Over One's Head

The opportunity for most people to obtain affordable, livable shelter is slowly slipping away. Neither commercial housing markets nor public housing projects are capable of solving the problems of the short supply, rising cost, and deteriorating quality of much of the world's housing stock. In the next few decades, individual efforts to construct or rehabilitate homes and cooperative ventures to rehabilitate and manage multi-family housing units will be an important avenue to better housing for the poor and for many members of the middle class.

The United Nations estimates that the number of households in the world will increase by 44 percent between

1970 and 1985. In urban areas alone, however, authorized
construction is expected to fall four to five million housing
units behind demand each year during that period. This housing shortfall comes at a time when at least 800 million people
are already living in badly built, badly equipped dwellings.[1]

The widening gap between demand and supply has led to
ever higher housing prices. In the United States, where the
average cost of a house exceeded $72,000 in 1979, home prices
rose faster than median incomes throughout the seventies and
were accelerating nearly twice as fast as incomes by the end of
the decade. In Japan, the cost of a house has nearly tripled in
the last ten years. World Bank data indicate that even the
cheapest housing units, publicly or privately built, are too expensive for one-third to two-thirds of the people in most developing countries. Those who can afford to buy do so at great
risk. Families must often commit a third to a half of their
disposable income to mortgage payments. Devoting so much
of its resources to housing severly limits a family's economic
options, and places it in a precarious financial position. These
are the new home-owning poor.[2]

The situation is also tightening for renters. Rent absorbs an
ever larger portion of the average renter's income. Moreover,
the supply of rental units is dwindling. The U.S. Department
of Housing and Urban Development (HUD) anticipates a
shortfall of 155,000 to 200,000 rental units per year in the next
decade. As demand outstrips supply, rents for those who are
fortunate enough to find an apartment will go even higher.[3]

Mounting competition for housing and rising costs are forcing ever growing numbers of the poor, the elderly, and minorities to move from their homes. While no reliable statistics on
the volume of displacement exist, sample data suggest that
one-quarter to one-third of all those who move from inner-city
areas in any given year in the United States are forced to do
so, largely by the influx of affluent people who are buying old
houses or converted apartments (condominiums).[4]

In the past, governments attempted to meet the needs for

shelter that private enterprise could not fulfill. Now, state-controlled housing projects face the same set of economic constraints that trouble the private sector. For example, in the late seventies the U.S. government built a public housing project called Taino Towers in New York's Spanish Harlem. Construction costs topped $60 million. Over the expected forty-year life of the project, these four 35-story towers will cost the government a total of $150 million for construction, upkeep, and interest, and possibly an additional $350 million in rent subsidies—all to house 656 families.[5]

Architect Tomasz Sudra's studies in Ismailia, Egypt, shed revealing light on how well-intentioned public efforts to improve housing often backfire, harming the very people they were meant to help. "It [Egypt's public housing policy] was a very inefficient policy," Sudra notes. "It provided very little housing for the funds invested, most of it did not go to the intended beneficiaries, and more important, it inhibited the massive normal housing process, greatly reducing its supply capacity . . . the more public housing was built, the less housing was built altogether."[6]

Intended as an enlightened way to move people out of the squalor of deteriorating tenements, public housing has often done no more than replace a horizontal slum with a vertical one. It is little wonder that governments are getting out of the housing business. In 1980, HUD built one-third fewer public housing units than it built in 1978; at the same time the United Kingdom began selling off its public housing units to the occupants, and Poland has abandoned government construction of houses altogether in favor of cooperatives where residents do much of the work.[7]

This, then, is the housing dilemma. Commercially constructed private homes and apartments are beyond the economic reach of more and more people. Public housing has often proved too expensive for the government that builds it and uninhabitable for the poor who rent it. One solution to this dilemma is for people to do more to help house themselves:

building houses from scratch, rehabilitating their own homes, or taking on added responsibilities as renters.

Self-help Housing

Until the mid–nineteenth century in Europe and North America, and until quite recently in Asia, Africa, and Latin America, most people built their homes themselves, or at least supervised the construction. Nearly two-thirds of all housing ever built was constructed in this way.[8] Reviving these traditions could help people to cope with spiraling housing costs.

Already, economic conditions are forcing people to fix up their old homes rather than buy new ones. Do-it-yourself rehabilitation, which begins whenever a person picks up some tools to repair a leaky roof or to fix a drafty window frame, was a $24-billion-a-year business in the United States in 1979. Since 1977, the value of self-help rehabilitation has equaled or exceeded the value of work done by professionals, reversing a two-decade-old trend. As this figure does not include the cost of personal labor, the addition to the value of the housing stock attributable to self-help activities is even greater.[9]

The actual number of houses and apartments rehabilitated each year by their owners is unknown. In the United States, for example, the Urban Land Institute estimates that between 1968 and 1975, 58,000 housing units were completely rehabilitated through private efforts in inner-city areas. This number has undoubtedly grown substantially since then, as rising prices for newly constructed homes have made older houses more attractive. While most of these homes were professionally redone, there has been a marked increase in homesteading, where resourceful people take vacant, decaying housing, often no more than a shell, and rebuild it from the inside out.[10]

Urban homesteading draws its inspiration from the American pioneer philosophy that occupation and improvement give rights to ownership. About 30,000 housing units are abandoned each year in American inner cities. With no more open spaces to settle, today's homesteaders have turned their eyes to these vacant homes. Houses that have become government property in lieu of back taxes are sold for a nominal sum, often no more than a dollar, to couples or individuals willing to move in and rebuild them. Occupants buy their homes with the investment of their own labor. Through U.S. government programs, such "sweat equity" had opened the door to homeownership for more than 3,500 homesteading families by the end of 1979. Additional houses were made available through city-sponsored programs. Although this figure is a mere drop in the bucket, it is a beginning. Meanwhile, there has been equal enthusiasm for homesteading where it has been tried in Europe; in London there were 11,000 applicants for the first 200 homesteads.[11]

The ultimate self-help housing is, of course, building one's own home from the ground up. Every year, over 200,000 families in the United States act as general contractors and oversee the design, financing, and construction of their homes. This sector has represented a stable one-fifth of the housing market since the mid-sixties.[12] As housing prices continue to rise, more and more people may have to resort to self-help housing to obtain a home of their own.

Cooperative Housing

Most people, however, are not able to secure shelter solely through their own efforts and resources. Self-help housing for the poor and for people with moderate incomes is ideally a cooperative effort, where friends and neighbors help each other to build, rehabilitate, or maintain their homes.

Nowhere is this more evident than in the squatter towns that surround the burgeoning cities of the Third World, where mutual aid often forms the backbone of the social structure. Older residents help new arrivals hastily erect cardboard shelters. Slowly, adobe or thatch walls replace the cardboard, and extra rooms are added. Part-time carpenters, plumbers, and bricklayers work for a modest fee or for traded labor. At least half of all housing work is done through these informal assistance networks and by local tradesmen.[13]

The use of "neighbor power" to provide or improve housing has recently been revived in industrial countries, to enable the poor to renovate their homes and fight displacement. Residents of the low-income Phillips area of Minneapolis, for example, started a self-help housing program in 1972 called the "Project for Pride in Living." Their efforts now include a tool lending library and construction training and employment programs for poor and minority residents. Similarly, in New Haven, Connecticut, some neighborhood groups have joined together to acquire and rehabilitate properties and to counsel residents interested in home improvement, housing maintenance, and energy conservation.[14]

The incentive to renovate and to maintain one's home is limited, however, if the house belongs to someone else. Ownership creates pride and a vested interest in both one's property and one's neighborhood. With this principle in mind, a priest working with neighborhood activists in Baltimore organized Saint Ambrose Housing Aid Center in 1972. The group has worked with low-income people to pressure lending institutions to help about 800 renters become homeowners. Saint Ambrose has organized its own real estate agency, which serves families with poor credit histories who are usually shunned by traditional real estate brokers. Once the pace of displacement in a particular neighborhood has been slowed, Saint Ambrose then helps people to rehabilitate their housing and to rebuild the economic base of their community.[15]

Many low-to-moderate income families living in apartment buildings are becoming interested in multi-family homesteading. This calls for the renovation of abandoned or rundown multi-unit buildings through the creation of self-help cooperatives, in which each participant gains equity through the contribution of his or her labor. For example, the Banana Kelly Community Improvement Association in the South Bronx requires that homesteaders put in 600 hours of free labor in order to obtain a co-op apartment.[16]

Many of the problems associated with public and private rental apartments, such as failure to pay rent and the high cost of maintenance, can be minimized when people are collectively responsible for their housing. Close tenant cooperation in apartment buildings—to agree on thermostat levels, to coordinate demand for hot water, or to caulk apartment windows —can lead to dramatic energy savings. By doing some of their own minor repairs, sweeping hallways, and taking out the trash, tenants can help keep down rent increases.

The possibility that self-help efforts could stem the rising costs of public housing led the Ford Foundation, in conjunction with the Department of Housing and Urban Development, to fund the National Tenant Management Demonstration in six U.S. cities from 1976 to 1979. Tenants were responsible for simple maintenance and rent collection. Although no clear pattern emerged, tenant management did no worse than conventional management, and in some cases outperformed it. In a similar program, New York City, which is the reluctant landlord of approximately 30,000 occupied apartments (as a result of tax foreclosures on slumlords), is turning over many of these properties to community management groups and tenants. The results have been encouraging; for example, while rent collection is only 45 percent in city-managed buildings, it is 80 percent in buildings managed by neighborhood housing groups, and 90 percent in tenant-managed buildings.[17]

The psychological dynamic at work in both private and publicly owned rental housing is the same. The most effective incentive for tenants to act responsibly is concern for what their neighbors will think. If a housing community can be created, one where everyone knows everyone else and depends on them, then a sense of common purpose can lead to better housing. As one resident of the Holloway Tenant Cooperative in the North Islington neighborhoods of London candidly ad-

mitted, "The last thing I want is to owe rent to the Co-op—
if it were any other landlord I'd make him wait. . . . I get
embarrassed about being in arrears and seeing Co-op workers."[18]

More than Housing

People build or rehabilitate their own housing in order to
have a roof over their heads. But self-help housing efforts
benefit society in other ways as well. The financial savings are
substantial. The Urban Homesteading Assistance Board of
New York City estimates that the cost of completely rehabilitating a two-bedroom housing unit through sweat equity averaged $15,000 in 1976. This compares to development costs of
approximately $32,000 for rehabilitation by a conventional
contractor, and $45,000 per unit for new construction. A study
by the advocacy group Rural America found that the migrant
workers and the rural poor who participate in the U.S. government's rural self-help housing program can build a home about
35 percent more cheaply than a contractor. Conversion of
multi-family rental units into cooperatives is up to 40 percent
cheaper than conversion into condominiums because there are
no middlemen. If some of the rehabilitation involved in the
conversion is done by the residents themselves, the savings can
be even greater.[19]

The same magnitude of savings is available in self-help projects in the Third World. Tomasz Sudra's housing studies in
Ismailia show that, for two-thirds of the population, traditional
self-help housing costs the equivalent of about three years of
average income. Low-priced commercial housing costs from
two to seven years of income. Public housing is the most
expensive. If its inhabitants were forced to pay for it directly,
public housing would cost from seven to twenty-two years of
income per home.[20]

Self-help rehabilitation also leads to energy and resource
savings. The energy used per square foot in rehabilitation is

about half that used in new construction. Recycling of old buildings saves energy in two ways: first, use of the existing walls and internal structure reduces the amount of material, and thus energy, needed to create a livable space; and second, rehabilitation often lends itself to the use of materials that require less energy to perform a given function. Moreover, older buildings, which were often designed to be compatible with their environments and to be naturally heated and cooled, can be rehabilitated to rely on many of these same solar properties, thus reducing their dependence on nonrenewable fuels.[21]

Recycling housing can also mean recycling neighborhoods. If, through their own efforts, the poor can avoid displacement, high-density urban neighborhoods can be preserved. If job opportunities can be expanded and neighborhood food and retail distribution systems rebuilt, there may be added energy savings as consumers are again centralized, able to walk to stores or to their jobs, and able to rely on mass transit rather than private automobiles for transportation. In the sprawling cities of the Third World, the upgrading of squatter settlements uses less energy and natural resources than relocating residents and building them new homes on the outskirts of town.

In a world where employment in the housing sector is an indicator of the health of the economy, the impact on the job market of greater individual and collective self-help housing is a matter of concern. Do-it-yourself repairs and home additions replace some hired labor, but they also create jobs. Two-fifths of the work done on government-funded self-help housing projects in rural areas of the United States is labor by electricians or plumbers who are hired to do work that people cannot do for themselves. Without the self-help activities, which account for the other three-fifths of the work, these jobs would never have been created.[22]

Similarly, in the Third World, self-help housing can help stimulate the local economy. Helping a neighbor build or rehabilitate a home is not recorded as official employment, but usually people are paid something or get help building their own homes in return. The support services for commercial construction generally come from outside the immediate community, while self-help builders draw on local stores and materials suppliers. Moreover, once a person has a home of his or her own, it can become a source of income. Most of the squatters in the Dandora settlement of Nairobi, for example, rent out rooms in their houses. It is not uncommon for Dandora householders to earn more money as landlords than they earn in wages.[23]

The sense of community cohesion that arises from collective self-help efforts can lead to other initiatives. In Lusaka, Zambia, for example, squatters have formed cooperative markets, credit unions, and rudimentary schools, and have created some of the most democratic and responsive branches of Zambia's only political party. These people remain desperately poor by any standard. But the sense of accomplishment that has come from controlling their own housing has begun to lead to political and economic control over other aspects of their lives.[24]

Helping People House Themselves

Governments are beginning to recognize the contribution people can make to meeting their own shelter needs, and the potential economic benefits of such efforts for the community. But public bodies can do much more to encourage and facilitate self-help housing.

The World Bank's "basic urbanization" project is the world's largest self-help housing program. Between 1972 and 1979, the Bank provided $926 million for self-help projects in more than fifteen countries.[25] Initially, the Bank's program consisted of "sites-and-services" projects, an approach to self-help housing that included the provision of a dwelling site, roads, water, and sewage disposal. It was assumed that after minimal preparation the sites could be turned over to poor

families who would have sufficient construction and maintenance skills to build themselves adequate housing. Unfortunately, it soon became clear that the cost to the Bank of such
a strategy—from $600 to $3,500 per dwelling—was prohibi-
tive. Applying it to the several hundred million squatters in the
world was out of the question. In addition, many sites-and-
services projects caused problems because they often uprooted
the poor and resettled them far from their jobs and from the
handicraft markets that provide their meager incomes. Such
difficulties led to a phasing out of the sites-and-services approach. It now makes up less than half of the World Bank's
urbanization program.

The Bank now spends most of its housing money on helping
people to upgrade their existing homes and providing them
with basic social services in their old communities. Self-help
housing assistance often costs no more than $200 to $300 per
dwelling, and it stimulates the local economy by drawing on
indigenous materials and labor. Individuals help build or renovate their own homes in almost every project. The Bank has
used cooperative self-help efforts as a means of expanding the
poor's control over community affairs. In a project to upgrade
the Tondo Foreshore region of Manila, residents were presented with three options for the realignment of houses and the
layout of roads, footpaths, and waterpipes. Final choices were
made by each neighborhood. In the Cockburn Gardens section
of Kingston, Jamaica, committees elected by the community
have full responsibility for public education, physical planning,
and management of upgrading.[26]

National and local governments in developed countries
could also do much more to support self-help housing.
Municipalities own some 300,000 abandoned dwellings in the
United States alone. Yet, until recently, relatively little effort
has been made to match up these homes with prospective
moderate-income homesteaders.[27]

Baltimore, where there has probably been as much homesteading as any city in the United States, is a good example of

what can happen when a government decides to stretch its housing dollars by wholeheartedly supporting homesteading. Fifteen years ago, Baltimore's economy was stagnating, its suburbs were growing, and many of its oldest neighborhoods were being abandoned. Fell's Point, Ridgeley's Delight, and Otterbein, whose streets lined with brick houses are Baltimore landmarks, were all targets for the wrecker's ball. An innovative self-help program has contributed to turning this situation around. The city participates in the federal homesteading program, and also makes $37,500 of local funds available in low-interest mortgage funds to each person willing to homestead abandoned city-owned properties. As a result, much of the community's unique architectural heritage has been preserved and homesteading has created an infectious enthusiasm for city living in Baltimore.[28]

Homesteading programs will require government subsidies if they are to reach low-income people. The mean income of homesteaders in U.S. federal programs is more than $12,000, which means that the programs have not reached the very poor. Many of the multi-family homesteading experiments in New York City with poorer participants have had trouble meeting their mortgage and tax payments.[29] By returning houses to the tax rolls and stimulating neighborhood economies, homesteading can generate new tax revenues, but governments will have to prime the pump.

Beyond official self-help programs, facilitating the acquisition of legal rights to land use is probably the single most important thing governments can do to foster self-help housing. For the squatter in Calcutta or the urban homesteader in the South Bronx, confidence that one's property will not be arbitrarily confiscated to build a freeway or industrial park is of paramount importance. This assurance is necessary if people are to make an extended commitment to better housing and to community development.

In cases where land tenure is out of the question, it is only just that the squatters own the structures and improvements they have made. The fact that a squatter is illegally occupying someone else's land should not give the landowner the right to tear down with impunity homes built with meager savings and years of hard work. Without compensation for such investments, squatters will have little incentive to start over again.

Since squatters occupy private and public land that they do not own, helping them to gain tenure challenges political and economic elites. This is a bold political step few governments have been willing to take. For this reason, it is crucial that community organizing go hand in hand with self-help housing efforts among squatters, so that political pressure can be brought to bear to expand the rights of the poor.

Government support for self-help housing can also include assistance in obtaining funds for construction and long-term financing. Banks usually will not lend to people with low incomes—the very people who have the most to gain from self-help housing. Governments can step in and provide the initial capital to guarantee mortgages. They can also help create institutions—such as credit unions—to mobilize the savings of those involved in self-help housing projects.

New tax laws can also encourage self-help housing. The Dutch Government rebates 40 percent of the cost of home improvements under $7,000, for example. Saint Louis, Missouri, and Newark, New Jersey, both give tax relief for housing rehabilitation.[30] Because self-help housing efforts can stimulate local economies, governments should consider tax relief based on the monetary value of rehabilitation work done by people with low incomes.

Governments can encourage self-help efforts as a means of improving neighborhood housing stock without causing displacement. This will require making tenant ownership easier by passing laws that give tenants the first right of refusal when landlords sell their homes. If this is coupled with public loans to low-income people doing self-help renovation, then opportunities will be created to revitalize inner-city neighborhoods without pushing out their long-time residents.

Laws to limit speculative buying and selling of government-assisted self-help housing can ensure that public funds do not end up benefiting the middle class. If publicly owned land is turned over to those who occupy and improve it, then any unearned increment in land value should accrue to the community and not to the newly tenured occupant. In this way government efforts to encourage self-help community development will not be short-circuited by individual profiteering. If this proves politically unfeasible, then some limitation should be placed on how fast newly tenured people can turn over property.

Inappropriate government housing standards can unnecessarily impede do-it-yourself work. In all too many cases, national and international lending agencies prescribe standards requiring that a wall must be of brick, so many inches thick, rather than that a wall, of whatever material, must insulate to a given degree and bear a given load. Specifications for performance rather than for components would allow self-help home builders or renovators to construct cheaper and more appropriate dwellings with skill and imagination. Such standards could rely on age-old local building techniques, which are more likely to be within the occupant's construction capabilities and resources, and also more suited to local climatic conditions.

Governments can do more than simply change laws or dip into their treasuries and their stock of abandoned housing to help people house themselves. They can participate in public/private partnerships to facilitate self-help at the local level. The U.S. Neighborhood Housing Services (NHS) is composed of neighborhood residents, local lenders, and city officials. NHS has set up high-risk revolving loan funds in several dozen cities to help residents at the lower end of the income spectrum to buy and rehabilitate their homes. The city government and local lenders agree to provide most of the money and the city agrees to upgrade services and housing inspections in the area. For its part, the federal government provides staff, training, and technical assistance. The people who live in the homes provide some sweat equity and the individual and collective initiative that holds all these divergent actors together. Through NHS, the U.S. government acts as the catalyst for self-help that might otherwise never happen.[31]

While governments should do all they can to encourage owner-built and -managed housing, they should be careful not to push people into responsibilities they cannot handle. For a variety of reasons—poverty, physical disability, age—many people may not want or be able to take greater control over their housing. For this reason, people need a range of housing options, including rental and public housing.

Yet the global slowdown in economic growth now forecast for the next few decades will mean that fewer and fewer people will be able to afford to buy or to rent commercially built housing, and that governments will not have the financial resources to house all those in need. As a result, that portion of the housing market that people build, renovate, or maintain themselves—and thus have some control over and responsibility for—will become increasingly important. In many ways, this development is desirable. For people are often their own best planners and builders—investing more time and labor in housing construction and improvement than any public or private developer can. And, as low-income housing consultant John Turner has pointed out, "When dwellers control the major decisions and are free to make their own contribution to the design, construction, and management of their housing, both the process and the environment produced stimulate individual and social well-being."[32]

5

Small Is Bountiful

In the last generation, much of humanity has broken its link with the soil. Severing this relationship has increased people's vulnerability to food shortages and rising prices. Today, a Russian peasant, an Indonesian rice farmer, and an American suburbanite all have less control over their food supply than did their ancestors.

The path to greater food security is not, of course, a return to people growing all their own food—an impractical, if not impossible, undertaking. But, by producing even a portion of the food that graces their tables people can build a buffer against inflation and malnutrition, while lessening the impact of state and corporate food policies on their lives.

During the fifties and sixties, world food production increased dramatically, and consumers bought more and more of
their food from commercial sources. In the United States, low
food prices, the appearance of convenience foods, and the
desire to shed "old-fashioned" ways nearly spelled the demise
of the home garden. In the Soviet Union, the cultivation of
private plots was discouraged when the opening up of new
agricultural lands led the government to believe that the country would soon become self-sufficient in food. In some developing countries, Indonesia for example, the poor abandoned their
kitchen gardens when the availability of high-yielding varieties
of rice held out the promise of abundant, cheap food.

The abandonment of home food production was a mistake,
because modern agriculture, although it is marvelously productive, has not been able to ensure low food prices and an adequate diet for everyone. Food prices in the United States have
risen at an annual rate of 9 percent since 1972. In the United
Kingdom and France, prices climbed 10 to 15 percent per year
during the seventies. But the sharpest impact of higher food
prices is being felt in developing countries, where basic staples
already account for more than half the family budget. In these
circumstances, rising prices have meant less food on the table.
As J. Dawson Ahalt of the U.S. Department of Agriculture has
pointed out, "The number of undernourished people in the
world has not been reduced in the past two decades, though
world grain production has increased 51 percent during that
time."[1]

Home Gardening

Throughout history, people have raised some of their food
in the immediate environs of the home. In ancient times,
urban Greeks planted quick-growing seeds of lettuce, wheat,
and barley in earthenware containers. The Romans often had
windowsill and balcony gardens.[2]

In recent years, concern about food prices, nutrition, and the quality of fruits and vegetables obtained from commercial sources has led to renewed interest in home food production. In the United States, the children of people who abandoned gardening in the immediate postwar years have enthusiastically returned to it. A Gallup Poll in 1979 showed that 42 percent of all households—33 million families—raise vegetables. To put this in perspective, more households now garden than enjoy recreations like fishing, bowling, or tennis.[3]

The popularity of gardening has followed the economic cycle. After food and energy prices increased in the early seventies, nearly half of all families planted a garden. Interest then tailed off until the end of the decade, when a new round of inflation led to a surge in gardening. The ultimate potential for home food production in the United States during times of increased need is difficult to assess accurately. However, a good yardstick may be that more than half the population had "victory gardens" during World War II.

In nine out of ten cases Americans raise their favorite vegetables—tomatoes, onions, and beans—in their own yards. Families that do not have yards are growing fruits and vegetables in the most ingenious places. A quick study of suburban apartment terraces or inner-city tenement fire escapes shows a surprising number of people growing peppers or tomatoes in milk cartons or flowerpots. Window gardening is a popular adjunct to tending houseplants. Greenhouses are sprouting on the sides of buildings from Maine to California. The adaptation of greenhouses to heat interior rooms has given some people the incentive to build these glass or plastic structures as combination gardens/solar heaters.

The home garden is an equally important aspect of life in many Third World countries. Actual data on the extent of gardening are scarce, although in many countries about one-third to one-half of the families garden. These home gardens can be marvelously complex, ecologically balanced arrangements. According to Karl Peltzer in a study of Indonesian gardens for the American Geographical Society, "The ground story consists of low-growing plants, especially tuberous plants that tolerate shade, such as . . . bitter cucumbers, gourds, lima beans. . . . The middle story taller-growing plants, such as cassava . . . papaya, banana. . . . The upper story is formed by tall fruit trees such as coconut . . . mango. . . ."[4]

School books in Java even refer to house-gardens as *warung hidup*, which is Javanese for "living food stalls." Since most of the plants are perennials, there is always some food to harvest, an important dietary supplement when the rice harvest may be one or two months away, and a source of income when money for daily houshold needs becomes scarce. The gardens also afford a ready supply of medicinal roots, herbs, and leaves that has led the Javanese to give these areas another name—*apotik hidup*, "living pharmacies."[5]

Community Gardening

The opportunities for home gardening, however, are often limited because people who want to garden have little or no access to land of their own. As early as the seventeenth century, European governments recognized this problem and allotted gardening plots on public land to urban peasants. Today there are more than a half million such allotments in England and Wales. These highly prized plots are often handed down from generation to generation and some have been in the same family for more than a century. Today, the demand for gardening space far exceeds the supply of land. The number of people on British waiting lists for a government-sponsored garden plot grew from less than 10,000 in 1969 to about 120,000 in 1977.[6]

On the Continent, interest in gardening is equally strong. Nearly 1.3 million West Germans belong to organized gardening groups that represent nearly one out of ten German families. Community gardeners use public and private land specifically set aside for them. Many German cities are ringed by garden plots rented out to city dwellers who commute to them in the evenings and on weekends. In Denmark, the Federation of Colony Garden Associations acquires land by purchase or long-term lease, lays out the gardens, and leases them to members. The gardens are elaborate affairs. Gas, water, and electricity are available for each plot. The entire colony may be set in parkland and surrounded by trees. Playing fields, a children's playground, and other community facilities are not uncommon.[7]

In the United States, community gardening has mushroomed in popularity in recent years. Gardens have developed in the most unlikely places—under freeways, along railroad rights-of-way, on abandoned farmland, and along river banks. An estimated two million people gardened on community plots in 1978 and an additional six million told pollsters they would garden if they had access to land. Once a few neighbors start gardening, enthusiasm for it can spread rapidly. Like many self-help efforts, the camaraderie, the enjoyment, and the practical benefits of gardening encourage others to join in.[8]

In Chicago, for example, the Housing Authority launched a community gardening program in 1971 as part of the city's beautification effort. This project has expanded and the produce grown now provides an important supplement to the diets of 6,000 families. The Los Angeles Neighborhood Gardens and Farms Program encompasses more than 2,000 families who collectively produce more than a million dollars worth of vegetables annually. The city provides a full-time staff of five gardening experts to help people throughout the community with their gardening problems.[9]

The community gardening movement has grown to encompass composting projects, greenhouses, canneries, and marketing. Urban agriculture has become an important building block in neighborhood revitalization, as community groups work together to create more green space in their neighborhoods, to provide recreation, and to grow cheap, nutritious food. Al Harris, leader of the New York City gardening program, sums up the attitude of many community garden organizers: "We not only grow vegetables, we grow hope." One payoff for communities with gardens is neighborhood solidarity. Weeding and hoeing side by side brings many neighbors together for the first time. They develop a spirit of cooperation and community pride. During the 1977 New York City blackout, which triggered so much random lawlessness, city blocks with community gardens suffered relatively little from looting. People in those neighborhoods say it was because everyone knew each other.

Small-scale food production in socialist countries is also a community endeavor. In the USSR, there are as many as 50 million private plots, a somewhat misleading term because these garden plots are on public land and much of the produce is not for personal consumption but for market sale. Most of these gardens are on state farms, but recent agricultural shortages have led to urban gardening activities on an unprecedented scale. A person flying over traditionally gray Soviet cities would now see them speckled with green garden plots. Soviet economist T. Khadonov reports that the land area devoted to private plots for urban workers and state employees now almost equals that of private plots on collective farms. As a result, collective gardening associations have blossomed, amateur seed hybridization societies have proliferated, and, for the first time in recent memory, state stores carry fertilizer and garden utensils.[10]

The magnitude of private plot production in the USSR dwarfs that of gardens in the West. In the United States, as little as 13 percent of all vegetables are home grown. In the Soviet Union in 1978, 61 percent of the potatoes and 29 percent of the other vegetables were produced on private plots.[11]

Gardening's Many Harvests

One measure of gardening's potential is the portion of a family's diet that can be grown in a given area in a limited amount of time. In most societies it will never be efficient to grow the most important calorie sources, wheat and rice, in the backyard. But fruits and vegetables are another story. An American family of four can produce between one-quarter and two-thirds of its vegetable consumption from a 600-square foot plot, by devoting about five hours per week to gardening over the summer.[12]

As these figures indicate, small-scale food production can be a productive way to use land and other resources. Yields can vary widely, however, depending on climate, the availability of water and fertilizer, and the individual gardener's expertise. Under near-laboratory conditions, Ecology Action of Palo Alto, California, has obtained yields of three pounds of vegetables per square foot of land. These results were obtained with French Intensive/Biodynamic gardening techniques, which include special preparation of the soil, composting, and companion planting. However, experiments by the Texas Agricultural Experiment Station in Renner, Texas, and Gardens for All in Burlington, Vermont, indicate that the average American gardener can expect to harvest no more than one pound of vegetables per square foot. In practice, many weekend gardeners produce even less. Yet these yields demonstrate that home production can be competitive with commercial vegetable production, which averages less than a half pound per square foot.[13]

Estimates of yields in other countries are more conservative. Kenneth R. Walker, in *Planning in Chinese Agriculture,* calculates that in the late fifties, a model garden in China produced three-quarters of a pound of produce per square foot, but that good land and intensive methods often raised yields to nearly a pound. A World Bank–funded gardening project in Colombia was based on expectations of only one-third of a pound of production per square foot. Such low yields suggest that there is still great potential for increasing home food production in the Third World.[14]

In these economically troubled times, garden produce can act as a buffer against rising food prices. Gardens for All estimates that the average American family with a garden was able to produce $367 worth of food in 1979, after expenses, enough to decrease its food bill by about 10 percent. U.S. Department of Agriculture studies suggest that for every hour spent in the garden, an individual gets a net return of three to five dollars. The financial advantages of gardening hold true in Europe as well. In Britain, for example, a family with an allotment cultivates approximately $300 worth of vegetables for an annual rental fee of $10 plus the cost of seeds and fertilizer.[15]

The economic significance of gardening and small-livestock-raising in socialist countries is far greater than in the West. According to official figures, private plots provide one-quarter of the income of families on Soviet collective farms. In the late fifties, as much as a third of Chinese family income, depending on the region of the country, came from private plots. This portion has since decreased, and may now represent only 15 to 20 percent of Chinese peasant earnings countrywide. Although much of this income comes from cash crops, such as tobacco, rather than food crops, self-help food production clearly complements the role of the socialist state in maintaining the Chinese standard of living.[16]

The importance of homegrown produce in the diet is evident in Indonesia, where home gardens account for 16 percent of the total daily food consumption in rural households. Nutrient-rich garden crops help balance diets that are often too dependent on starchy foods. Carrots and cabbage, for example, can provide Vitamin A and calcium, in contrast to rice and potatoes, which contain no Vitamin A and only minute quantities of calcium.[17]

Gardening's bounty not only bolsters human energy; gardening can also save substantial amounts of nonrenewable energy resources. In the United States, for example, processed vegetables require three times as much energy to grow, transport, and prepare as fresh vegetables. Substituting garden-grown foods for processed ones cuts out the energy middleman. Moreover, as gasoline prices increase, it makes less and less sense to transport lettuce or tomatoes 3,000 miles from California to Massachusetts, even if they are eaten raw, when there is untapped potential for local food production.[18]

Gardening also enables society to substitute under-utilized labor for money spent on food. As writer Catherine Lerza notes in discussing Hartford, Connecticut's extensive community gardening program, "Food production, processing and distribution . . . substitutes the labor of Hartford residents for the labor of Western farmworkers, crosscountry truckers and local warehousers, and supermarket checkers," thus channeling, at a considerable savings, some of the surplus labor of underemployed Hartford residents into the provision of services for themselves.[19] In parts of the Third World, where only one person in ten is engaged in regular wage labor, gardening can be an important economic activity that contributes a crucial part of the food supply, even though the activity may never be measured in the country's gross national product.

Finally, some of the most important rewards of home food production are intangible. Home garden produce is fresher and tastier than that commonly found in the supermarkets and it is less likely to have been sprayed with pesticides that pose long-term health hazards. Moreover, raising fruits and vegetables is a practical lesson in environmental education that no textbook can rival. For many people, working the earth on a small scale is a way to maintain traditional family connections with farming. The U.S. Gallup Poll on gardening indicates that many people garden for recreation and exercise, to get some earth under their fingernails, and to work up a sweat on a warm spring day. For others it is a form of therapy, a way to get back in touch with nature. And any gardener will testify to the personal satisfaction of sitting down to a homegrown meal.

Gardening as Food Policy

No government has given home food production the secure and prominent place in food and nutrition policy it deserves.

Dwarfed by the magnitude of farm production, gardening is still seen by most public officials as a marginal, if not frivolous, self-help activity that can largely be ignored. The failure of large-scale agricultural production to meet the food needs of the poor, the projections of ever higher food prices in years to come, and the growing concern about nutritionally balanced diets all dictate a rethinking of official policies toward gardening.

Probably the single most important thing governments can do to encourage home food production is to ensure that gardeners have access to land. Obviously, everyone who lives in crowded cities cannot have a garden. But Colin Hines, in a report for the British branch of Friends of the Earth, estimates that there is enough unused land in London alone to provide over 100,000 garden plots. A study by the Science Council of Canada suggests that there are about 174 square feet of potential garden land per person in the cities of Canada's two most densely populated provinces, Quebec and Ontario. This is enough space to provide about half the families in those cities with good-sized gardens.[20]

In the United States, many cities have acres of vacant land. If only the once-occupied but now abandoned land were converted into gardens, leaving parks and other green space untouched, Baltimore and New Orleans, for example, could create 10,000 new garden plots, Cincinnati, 22,500, and Cleveland, 50,000. In these cities, an additional 5 to 30 percent of the families could then have gardens.[21]

No city government has as yet systematically assessed its potential gardening space and attempted to match up interested gardeners with available land. One promising attempt to deal with this problem though is New York City's "Operation Green Thumb," which allows any citizen to garden on city-owned vacant lots, with minimum red tape and a token payment of one dollar. Community groups in several British cities have not waited for the government to act but have begun their own garden loan schemes, in which those wishing to garden trade some produce for the right to cultivate small plots of land owned by people who do not garden. Governments can also encourage private landowners to permit gardening and small livestock raising on their property by changing tax policies, zoning restrictions, and insurance regulations.

Just like farmers, gardeners want land tenure. They are reluctant to invest much time or money in building up the soil, improving the water supply, or constructing a tool shed if they cannot be sure of continued access to the land they till. Unfortunately, less than 5 percent of community gardening land in the United States is legally secure. One way the state can help gardeners, therefore, is to encourage the creation of neighborhood land trusts, like those in Oakland, California, and Newark, New Jersey, where local groups acquire title to garden plots and hold them in trust for the community.[22]

Once land has been secured, gardeners often need a little money to get started. Even a few dollars may be beyond the means of those who stand to benefit most from raising their own food. Since 1976, the U.S. government has funded urban gardening programs. The effort is run by the Department of Agriculture and is coordinated by the Land Grant Universities and county agricultural extension agents. Originally budgeted for $1.5 million in six cities, the program has been expanded to embrace sixteen cities and now has a $3 million budget. In 1978, federal gardening initiatives involved more than 88,000 people, mostly from low-income groups.[23] As urban residents learn gardening techniques and slowly improve the soil, gardening could become an efficient way for the government to help low-income people supplement their food budgets.

There is much that governments can do to facilitate gardening, at little or no public expense. Pennsylvania makes land available to gardeners on the grounds of state hospitals. The state has arranged for gardeners to get seeds at discount prices and encourages counties to make additional land available to local groups. The Pennsylvania program required no new legislation or budgetary appropriations. Participants provide their own materials or depend on donations from local merchants. This reliance on local initiative is a model of government support for self-help activities like gardening.

Socialist governments have long held inconsistent attitudes about small-scale private food production, at times treating it as an ideological pariah and at other times encouraging it. Whenever agricultural production lags, restrictions on private plots are eased. The most recent turnaround in Soviet policy in favor of private plots came in 1977, when President Leonid Brezhnev publicly stated that local officials should put aside philosophical misgivings and support private plot production because the economy needed the produce. Government loans were made available to improve plots and to buy livestock. In China, the revised constitution adopted in 1978 gave commune members the right to "farm small plots of land for personal needs, engage in limited household side-line production; and in pastoral areas they may also keep a limited number of livestock for personal needs." The legal maxium amount of village land that may be devoted to private production has been raised from 5 to 15 percent, although recent reports indicate that this has yet to be achieved.[24]

Throughout the Third World, increasing the food supply will ultimately require land reform and the adoption of more productive agricultural technologies. But in the short run, the most expedient way of achieving better diets may be to increase home food production, since gardening does not present the distribution difficulties inherent in mass-production agriculture. For example, in the early seventies, Jamaican farmers faced an unpleasant double bind—soaring prices for their food imports and a declining market for bananas, their principal crop. There was little slack in family budgets to absorb rising costs and declining income. Many families already spent more than three-quarters of their earnings on food. To stave off widespread malnutrition and political unrest, the government began a "Grow Our Own Food" campaign. In the rural Saint James Parish the portion of households using homegrown food increased from 38 to 56 percent between 1973 and 1975. The portion of income spent on food stabilized and child malnutrition dropped significantly.[25]

Successful gardening programs can be a homegrown problem, however, if there is no way to market the produce. Providing opportunities for gardeners to sell their excess produce would encourage full production, and enable nongardeners to buy fresh food. Hartford, Connecticut, has designed a comprehensive city food plan that includes community gardens, markets, and public canning facilities. In its first fifteen weeks of operation in 1978 the Hartford market had 60,000 customers. Nearly two dozen state governments in the United States now subsidize farmers' markets that could easily be expanded to allow gardeners to sell their extra produce, either directly or through some kind of cooperative. Marketing assistance for private growers and liberalization of restrictions on rural markets have been an integral part of Soviet and Chinese efforts to increase private plot production in recent years.[26]

The success of government gardening programs will be measured by their sensitivity to the gardening needs of people in different regions and economic groups. Agricultural extension services have neglected horticulture for too long. The federal gardening program in the United States has encountered problems because the Department of Agriculture extension agents used in the program are more at home on a thousand-acre wheat farm in Kansas than on a vacant lot in a ghetto neighborhood.

On the other hand, some of the most effective horticultural extension work is being done by local villagers and neighborhood residents who distribute seeds, give gardening advice, and generally promote home food production. The state gardening program in Benin, for example, is run through the Women's Club in each village. In Senegal, gardening programs that work through women's groups not only improve nutrition but give women new status. "Now that I have made some money, he [her husband] shows more respect for me," notes Anna

Basulco, leader of one Senagalese women's gardening collective. Twenty-one American states have established master gardener programs, where neighborhood residents are given a modicum of training to upgrade their already substantial gardening skills, in return for which they act as unpaid horticultural experts for their community.[27]

It will not be sufficient to create an interest in gardening, however, if nutritional ignorance and food taboos keep people from eating balanced diets. In Indonesia, for example, some villages have widespread anemia simply because iron-rich vegetables such as spinach are not grown in the community. The commercial cost of certain foods—such as meat, eggs, and vegetables, which could be home-produced—have often led them to be classified as nonessential by folk cultures. Food prejudices often exclude important resources from the diet. For reasons long forgotten, taboos sometimes keep Vitamin-A-rich vegetables away from children with eye problems. These nutritional values can best be changed in the way that they were formed, through information and peer pressure passed through social networks at the village level. Organized nutrition education programs that work through the traditional sources of nutritional information in the community can create new nutritional norms and enshrine in dietary custom the importance of certain horticultural products.[28]

Finally, a simple but often neglected step that governments can take to promote home food production is to scrutinize their own policies to identify obstacles to gardening. In the sixties, for example, the Soviet government initiated a policy of building apartments to house workers on collective and state farms, with disastrous consequences. With no land around their homes, these apartment dwellers had little opportunity to grow their own food. When a decline in private production resulted, the Soviet government soon mended its ways. Similarly, in Tanzania, the much publicized system of collective *Ujamaa* villages originally left little room between houses for gardens. Eventually, numerous towns were totally rebuilt so that each household could have enough kitchen-garden space to meet its basic needs.[29]

However, there are some obstacles to gardening that governments will find difficult to overcome. The availability of water around homes is cited by many experts familiar with gardening in developing nations as the single most important constraint on expanding home food production. Self-help projects to dig wells and lay water pipes will often be necessary to complement gardening programs. And many poor families may simply not have the time to devote to gardening. Subsistence living is a full-time activity for the poor, and expecting them to spend additional hours in the garden may often be unrealistic.[30]

Despite these constraints, however, people should have the opportunity to produce some of their own food if they choose to do so. In inflationary times, raising vegetables or fruits can enable families to gain some control over their food budget. Gardening can provide an important supplement to the diet, which in some developing countries may mean the difference between life and death. Such self-help efforts can improve a family's food security, an incremental but important first step toward world food security.

6

Taking Responsibility for Health

Two major health concerns dominate people's lives: how long they will live, and how often they will be sick. Ever greater investments in hospitals, drug research, and medical technology are increasingly irrelevant to these interests. Moreover, current reliance on this kind of health care has already created a burgeoning medical bill that threatens to bankrupt medical care in many countries.

In the future, health and longevity will, of necessity, depend on individuals and communities taking greater responsibility for their own health problems. In industrial countries, this will mean changes in personal living habits and greater reliance on self-care. In developing countries, it will include improved access to simple medical care, and preventive health measures aimed at the sources of disease.

Health and Health Care

People who live in modern industrial societies smoke too much, eat too much, and exercise too little. They drive too fast, they work too hard, and they worry too much. Their cities are often dangerously polluted. As a result, illnesses and deaths related to unhealthy habits and to an unhealthy environment are on the rise. Diseases of the heart and the circulatory system are prevalent, accounting for half of the deaths in affluent societies. Even in China, in some urban areas, heart attacks and strokes are now the leading cause of death. The U.S. National Cancer Institute estimates that one in four Americans will develop cancer. Accidents are the leading threat to life for Americans under the age of thirty-five. A study by the Canadian Ministry of Health asserts that "self-imposed risks and the environment are the principal or important underlying factors in each of the five major causes of death between age 1 and age 70."[1]

These disease and mortality patterns are associated with unhealthy practices that can be changed, but this fact has been disregarded until recently. "Prevention is both cheaper and simpler than cure, but we have stressed the latter and we have ignored, to an increasing degree, the former. . . . In effect, we've made the hospital the first line of defense instead of the last," noted President Jimmy Carter in a 1977 speech to the American Public Health Association.[2]

Chronic illness has also emerged as a major health care burden. Lowell Levin of Yale University estimates that forty years ago chronic illness represented only 30 percent of all diseases suffered by Americans. Today it represents 80 percent. More than 30 million people suffer from chronic conditions, like asthma, diabetes, and hypertension, that are severe enough to limit activity. By definition, these illnesses cannot be cured, but must be treated for years at great cost to individuals and to society. As prosperity and modern medicine reduce the threat of infectious diseases, the health care systems of more and more countries will face the challenge of long-term care of chronic illnesses.[3]

In North America and Europe, medical care systems are already burdened by needless dependence on doctors and hospitals. Several studies in Britain and the United States have shown that at least one-quarter of all visits to doctors were for conditions that people could care for themselves.[4] Rising affluence, the expansion of medical insurance coverage, and government-funded medical care have discouraged self-treatment of mundane illnesses. The treatment of normal human experiences—like anxiety or childbirth—is now the prerogative of professionals. People have become too dependent on costly psychiatrists or obstetricians for services that their ancestors obtained from lay practitioners—such as ministers or midwives —in their local communities.

Moreover, many people regard doctors as shamans who can magically cure them of their ills. The impressive record of medical breakthroughs over the last hundred years has led to expectations that doctors can conquer pain and somehow postpone death indefinitely. An attitude has developed in affluent countries that pain and discomfort are to be avoided at all costs. Colds, headaches, and minor injuries, which were inconveniences that people at one time tolerated, now merit full-scale medical intervention.

In developing countries, most health problems are also linked with conditions that can be prevented. Calorie-, protein-, and vitamin-deficient diets are the most important cause of illness among the underprivileged. Moreover, millions of babies are born weak and never survive infancy because women who have little access to family planning services are unable to space their childbearing. And, encouraged by formula manufacturers to bottle-feed their babies, mothers in developing countries are abandoning breast-feeding in droves, which, as

Cornell University physician Michael C. Latham observes, is "tantamount to signing the death certificate of the child."[5]

These emerging health care problems have contributed to burgeoning medical bills throughout the world. In the United States, health care costs increased from 5.2 percent to 9.1 percent of the gross national product (GNP) in the last decade. Between 1966 and 1976, the portion of the West German GNP devoted to medical care rose from 4.8 percent to 8 percent. Fragmentary evidence suggests that developing countries spend 6 to 10 percent of their gross domestic product on health care. Given competing demands for resources, it is unlikely that countries will be able to continue to expand their commitments to the medical sectors of their economies. A more cost-effective method for providing health services is essential.[6]

"An Ounce of Prevention"

Prevention has always been the neglected stepsister of health care. There has been little sense of urgency about prevention; careers devoted to it seem to many health professionals to be unrewarding and unexciting, for prevention often calls for simple solutions, while the human mind thrives on designing complex ones. Only one dollar in twenty that Americans spend on health care goes toward the prevention of illnesses; a paltry investment considering the potential benefits to be derived from such action. Preventive efforts, not medical treatment, were responsible for most of the improvement in life expectancy over the last century, according to historian Thomas McKeown.[7] Activities to maintain and improve personal health are no less important today.

In affluent countries, for example, the most important thing people can do for their health is to change their eating habits. The U.S. National Cancer Institute suggests that Americans could reduce their chances of succumbing to cancer by eating less fat, drinking less alcohol, eating more fiber, and watching their weight. Similar dietary changes could also help prevent heart disease. Recent improvements in American eating habits are encouraging evidence that people can be inspired to change their unhealthy diets. The average level of cholesterol in the blood of adults is declining. Americans eat fewer eggs, drink less whole milk, consume less candy, and put less butter on their toast than they did in the forties. During the same period, the consumption of cholesterol-free and polyunsaturated vegetable oils and margarine has more than doubled.[8]

Like poor nutrition, a sedentary life-style contributes to ill health. But through vigorous cardiovascular exercise people can become the masters of their fates and the captains of their hearts. Studies of the health and exercise histories of 17,000 Harvard University alumni indicate that as exercise levels increase up to the equivalent of running twenty miles a week at a moderate pace, the likelihood and the severity of heart attacks decrease. The prospect of living longer and feeling healthier has led to an exercise explosion. Between 10 and 40 million Americans jog regularly. On almost any morning in the Bois de Boulogne in Paris, people can be seen "footing," the French term for jogging. And at noon in Tokyo, joggers in colorful warm-up clothes run four abreast along the path around the Imperial Palace moat.[9]

The health benefits of not smoking are also well established. Studies have shown that nonsmokers are at least ten times less likely than cigarette smokers to develop lung malignancies, and nonsmokers under the age of sixty-five are half as likely as smokers to die of coronary heart disease. This evidence has convinced many people to stop smoking. Since major studies in the early sixties first linked smoking to serious illness, an estimated 29 million Americans have quit. In Britain, the proportion of men who smoke cigarettes fell from about 52 percent in 1973 to 45 percent in 1978.[10]

Mounting scientific evidence demonstrates that such changes in dietary, exercise, and smoking habits can have a significant impact on health. In the United States, the coro-

nary heart disease death rate has decreased by 11 percent since
1968. The U.S. Department of Health, Education, and Welfare links this achievement to declines in such cardiovascular
risk factors as hypertension, cigarette smoking, consumption of
saturated fats, and physical inactivity. A study of 7,000 adults
in California showed that those who lived longer and healthier
lives got adequate rest, ate three meals a day, exercised, did not
smoke, and did not eat or drink too much. The Harvard alumni
study indicates that if people can be encouraged to stop smoking, to exercise regularly, and to lower their blood pressure,
they can cut by half their risk of having a heart attack. Other
research suggests that similar life-style changes could save more
lives among the middle-aged than any conceivable advances in
medical science.[11]

The economic savings of people taking better care of themselves could be substantial. The medical bill for cardiovascular
disease in the United States in 1975 was $16 billion. In the
same year, cancer cost an additional $5.3 billion. Every heart
attack that can be prevented will save at least $7,500; similarly
every case of cancer that can be prevented will save $20,000
in hospital, physician, and drug costs. Few investments in
medical technology are as cost effective as self-help preventive
activities.[12]

Self-help efforts could also begin to provide the solution to
many health problems in developing countries. For example,
the produce from a kitchen garden can help overcome nutritional deficiencies and related diseases. Before the "Grow Our
Own Food" campaign in Saint James Parish in Jamaica, one
in every ten children in rural areas was seriously malnourished.
Two years later, after a sharp increase in home food production, the number of children suffering from severe malnutrition
had dropped to one out of twenty.[13] Similarly, breast-feeding
provides infants with adequate nutrition and initial protection
against disease. It is a natural activity that almost any mother
can engage in, one that could significantly lower infant mortality in developing countries.

Effective family planning ranks with good nutrition as a prerequisite for good health. Women with access to contraception and legal abortion can generally time and space their childbearing safely. Studies in Thailand indicate that women who can confine their childbearing to their twenties are only half as likely to die in childbirth as women who have babies too early or too late in life. Moreover, a study in Punjab, India, indicates that infants born two to four years apart have a one-third better chance of living past age one than infants born less than two years apart. By practicing family planning, women in the Third World can do more to improve maternal and infant health than any conceivable advance in medical care can.[14]

Yet the individual cannot bear the sole responsibility for better preventive health care. Even the most well-informed and financially independent person may be unable to assess the health impact of a particular life-style, or may fall victim to the blandishments of advertising or be confused by seemingly innocuous traditional practices. Ingrained habits are difficult to break, especially when individuals must bear the psychological burden alone. Many things detrimental to one's health, like food additives and toxic substances in the environment, are beyond personal control. Often the most effective way for people to confront a health problem is to work with their friends and neighbors to help each other to change unhealthy habits, to deal collectively with environmental conditions that contribute to illness, or to organize political pressure on governments to change dangerous conditions.

In the mid-seventies, a Stanford University team led a community-oriented effort to reduce the factors linked to heart disease in three California towns by changing eating and smoking habits. An orchestrated campaign of public information and peer pressure blended the use of mass media, face-to-face instruction, and community meetings. In one town, groups of a dozen or so persons met in local church halls to share a nutritious meal, to talk with a dietician, and to wage friendly competition in losing weight. A smoking therapist visited people in their homes to help them quit smoking. The results were encouraging. Fewer cigarettes were smoked, the consumption of saturated fats declined, and the blood pressure of those tested was reduced. Although it will take some time to demonstrate a decline in cardiovascular mortality, all these changes suggest that those who participated have one-quarter to one-third less risk of dying of cardiovascular disease.[15] Moreover, new community values were created that will reinforce people's efforts to live healthier lives.

A similar community effort to alter diet and smoking habits through public education and motivation began in 1972 in North Karelia, a rural county in eastern Finland. Studies had shown that proportionally more people died of heart disease there than anywhere else in the world, a dubious notoriety that inspired people to change their life-styles. In the first three years of the campaign, the proportion of men who smoked fell from 54 to 41 percent, and the proportion of those with high blood pressure declined from 39 to 34 percent. The consumption of low-fat milk tripled, and the consumption of butter declined by one-fourth. Similar dietary and smoking changes were noted during the same period in other parts of Finland, so it is difficult to assess the precise impact of the North Karelia program. However, it is clear that the participants' health improved. The heart disease rate among males decreased, as did the percentage of deaths due to stroke. "This means 100 less strokes a year," said Pekka Pushka, leader of the project. "In treatment saved we have more than paid for the whole eight-year North Karelia project."[16]

In the Third World, there is an equal need for community-based preventive health efforts. The Chinese program to eradicate schistosomiasis, a snail-borne parasitic disease that afflicted more than ten million Chinese as recently as 1955, is a textbook example of such efforts. In a series of collective activities, lasting from one day to several weeks, peasants spent literally millions of hours clearing irrigation canals and water sources of the snails that carry schistosomiasis and recycling human waste to make sure that the parasite does not get back into the water supply. While medical researchers in other countries still search for a safe and effective cure for schistosomiasis, the Chinese, through their simple preventive efforts, have all but eliminated it in two-thirds of the counties where it was once prevalent.[17] Similar community preventive health efforts are needed throughout the Third World to build latrines, to dig wells, to clean up mosquito-infested swamps, and to kill disease-carrying rats.

In their efforts to deal with health problems, communities will often have to exert political pressure to persuade governments to take a more active role in protecting the health of all citizens. In the mid-seventies, one West Side Chicago neighborhood learned this lesson when it decided to do something about traffic accidents. The incidence of accidents increased when several of the streets through the neighborhood became major thoroughfares for automobiles, as the result of decisions made in City Hall. While neighborhood residents could do some things to improve traffic safety, such as erecting cautionary signs, this health problem was largely out of their control. Local organizations eventually banded together with civic groups from all across Chicago to assemble enough political power to force city officials to change traffic patterns.[18]

Political mobilization around environmental health and safety issues is also necessary in the workplace and in neighborhoods surrounding polluting factories. Community organizing in the late seventies by the families who lived near the Love Canal chemical dump in Niagara Falls, New York, was instrumental in bringing to public attention the question of the health hazards of toxic substances. Government and industry experts repeatedly assured residents that the chemicals that were oozing out of their backyards were benign. But citizens were able to chronicle an abnormally high incidence of birth defects in the area. Using the media to publicize their plight, the citizen's association was able to force a government-sponsored evacuation of the area. As these cases demonstrate, the exercise of political power around health issues is often one of the most effective preventive health care measures.

In the decades ahead, prevention will be in the vanguard of a new public health revolution. In the Third World this revolution will be aimed at cleaning up water supplies, improving nutrition, and increasing the use of family planning. In industrial nations it will promote healthier habits and strive to prevent common diseases. Both revolutions will require, in the words of the U.S. Surgeon General's *Report on Health Promotion and Disease Prevention*, "a partnership that involves the serious commitment of individual citizens, the communities in which they live, the employers for whom they work, voluntary agencies, and health professionals."[19]

A Self-care Cure

A healthy life-style and a healthy environment will not completely eliminate the need for medical care. When that need arises, however, the first recourse can be to determine how much one can do to care for oneself. Most illnesses run their course with no life-threatening complications. Common sense and traditional home remedies are often sufficient cures.

Studies in England, Sweden, and the United States show that between two-thirds and three-quarters of the illnesses people experience are self-treated. For the most part, this treatment seems to be effective. Five out of ten people who go to a general practitioner have already begun self-prescribed treatment that is beneficial 60 to 80 percent of the time, according to reviews of office visits in Denmark and Great Britain.[20]

The public is slowly beginning to realize that traditional self-care practices are a health resource they can control. About five million people in the United States now belong to self-help groups dealing with health issues or psychological problems. Some join to change unhealthy personal habits, others to find a supportive community to help them cope with their problems; all are part of mutual aid support systems that are the fastest-growing means of providing human services in many countries.[21]

This self-help philosophy is abundantly clear in the work of Alcoholics Anonymous (AA). In daily and weekly meetings, small groups of AA members talk about themselves and their drinking problems. New friendships are formed without the lubrication of alcohol, and through the reinforcement of these friends, people slowly begin to change the way they perceive themselves and their need for liquor. *The Journal of the American Medical Association* reports that AA has been very successful in helping drinkers in their daily struggle with their disease: "Of those members sober less than a year, 35 percent will not drink. Of those sober one to five years, about 80 percent will not drink. . . ." A survey of general practitioners in England and Wales showed that two-thirds felt AA had something more to offer alcoholics than they themselves could provide.[22]

In recent years, groups of women dealing with their own gynecological concerns have constituted another significant element of the self-help medical movement. The idea is an old one. There were "women's clubs" for health education in fifteenth-century Venice, and women were active in the popular health movement in the United States in the 1830s and 1840s. Helen I. Marieskind of the State University of New York estimates that today there are more than 1,200 women's groups and at least fifty clinics run by women for women in the United States alone, and growing numbers of them in other countries. Women who attend these clinics are taught to examine their own cervices and breasts for possible precancerous conditions and to do their own pregnancy testing. The clinics run by women generally employ physicians, but patients deal mainly with nonprofessional women who have learned their skills in self-help courses.[23]

Surveys of women seeking medical care have found that those attending self-help clinics better understand female anatomy than women attending other types of medical facilities.

These women can also identify more clearly the common health problems that arise with contraceptive use. For some women, the cheaper cost of attending one of these clinics is important. But the main dividend of the women's health movement is increased understanding and thus the ability to take responsibility for one's body. This responsibility entails freedom of choice regarding such medical decisions as the selection of a contraceptive or the alternatives to psychoactive drugs in dealing with natural female conditions like menopause.

Mental disorders now afflict 15 percent of the American public in any given year. While some psychological problems require professional care, there is growing recognition that others can be handled with the help of friends and neighbors. The breakup of families and the decline of cohesive neighborhoods have contributed to the alienation that is at the root of much mental illness, and have weakened the community support networks that people have traditionally turned to in times of stress. Recognizing this situation, the U.S. President's Commission on Mental Health has recommended that public support of mental health services should focus on formal and informal helping networks as a way to improve the effectiveness of mental health care.[24]

Psychiatrist James G. Gordon estimated for the Commission that in the United States there are already more than 2,000 hotlines and 200 runaway houses that depend mainly on nonprofessional activists to provide most of their care. The little hard data available suggest that in many cases these groups provide care that is equal or superior to that offered by professional mental health centers, and at a much lower cost. Case studies show that the rehospitalization rate of chronic schizophrenics who were treated by nonprofessional community networks was cut in half, and those who were rehospitalized spent less time back in institutions than schizophrenics who were treated by formal mental health agencies.[25]

The medical establishment is beginning to recognize that

people with chronic diseases can often do much to take care of themselves. Organized self-care programs, often staffed by people who suffer from the same illness and with whom patients can easily identify, are proving to be successful and cost-effective replacements for professional medical supervision. A self-care program for diabetics run by the University of Southern California Medical Center, for example, reduced the number of patients experiencing diabetic coma by two-thirds, and saved hospitals and patients $1.4 million over a two-year period. In test self-care programs with hemophiliacs at the Tufts New England Medical Center, total costs per patient were lowered by 45 percent.[26] These examples represent a tiny fraction of the savings that could be realized if self-care for chronic illnesses was expanded.

There is, however, legitimate concern within the medical community that if self-care is encouraged, people will mistreat themselves. A little knowledge can be a dangerous thing. Yet, studies of people who have taken self-care courses, or who follow self-care manuals, indicate that they are well aware of when and how to use the medical system.[27]

Self-care is certainly not a replacement for all types of medical services, but it is a useful complement to an already over-taxed health care system. Although it is impossible to estimate precisely the potential cost savings from self-care, several billion dollars could be cut from the U.S. medical care budget through extensive reliance on simple self-care practices.

Self-care has an even more important role to play in the lives of people in rural areas of developing countries, where there are few or no organized medical services. They have long treated their own illnesses, identifying the symptoms, selecting the appropriate indigenous medical resource that has proved effective in the past, and applying the remedy. An estimated 65 to 90 percent of those who fall ill in South and Southeast Asia use largely self-administered herbal cures. Much of this self-care is worthless or dangerous. But, as Halfdan Mahler, director general of the World Health Organization, points out, "Modern

medicine has a great deal to learn from the collector of herbs
. . . there is no doubt that the judicious use of herbs, flowers
and other plants . . . can make a major contribution towards
reducing a developing country's drug bill." The efficacy of
traditional cures is only beginning to be understood by Western medical science. Studies in Chad, for example, have recently shown that traditional self-care by lepers is more effective than the efforts of the organized medical system.[28]

The first aim of government health care strategies in developing countries should be to identify and support the most
effective of these indigenous health care resources. But the
health needs of the poor cannot be met solely through greater
reliance on traditional care; if villagers in India or Upper Volta
are to live longer, healthier lives, they need better medical care
than their ancestors received. Self-care is only the foundation
upon which to build a community-based primary medical care
system staffed by paraprofessional health workers.

New Health Policies

There are ongoing debates in the United States and Europe
about the social implications of health care reform. Many
radical critics of modern health care systems caution that em-
phasis on prevention and self-care could serve as an excuse to
cut back on services for the poor. They say that self-help
activities "blame the victim" of disease, when it is really poverty that is the cause. They point out that historically it is the
poor who have higher death and disease rates. They contend,
for example, that inadequate nutrition is largely the result of
income disparities and of manipulative advertising, not of personal choice. "Discussing changes in life-styles without first
discussing the changes in the social conditions which give rise
to them . . . is misleading," argues Howard S. Berliner of Johns
Hopkins University.[29]

The questions Berliner and others raise strike at the very
heart of the issue of how human beings improve conditions in
society. Does one try to change the social and economic system

first, or change people first? Is lung cancer the result of a personal decision to smoke, or is it caused by the stress of modern life and the advertising that encourages people to smoke? Clearly, society should do more to curb the power of tobacco companies to promote an unhealthy habit, but millions of Americans have quit smoking without drastic changes in the system. People *can* begin to alter their fates through activities that are not overtly political.

Self-care and preventive health care can, however, be at the forefront of progressive social action. Efforts toward increased self-care might well take their lead from the women's health movement, and combine the provision of health services and education with an ongoing struggle to change health care institutions.

Such activities will necessarily involve the government. Government needs "a philosophy that health is not just something which is provided for by the N.H.S. (National Health Service), but that each individual has a responsibility for his own well-being," declared British Minister of Health David Owen in 1976. "It is not the role of government to dictate life-styles," U.S. President Jimmy Carter has cautioned, "but it is the proper role of government to educate our citizens and to aggressively stress the promotion of good health . . . the fact is, that if we were to improve our national eating, drinking, and smoking and exercise habits, we could be healthier, be happier, live longer, and save ourselves billions of dollars in the process."[30]

Governments can use various means to encourage cost-saving, health-preserving, self-help activities. Unhealthy foods or products can be taxed, and the proceeds used for preventive education. In countries with national health insurance, self-care courses might be required, like driver's licenses. Such programs could help create a public awareness that many modern diseases are the result of unhealthy habits, and also help decrease excessive reliance on the medical system for the treatment of simple illnesses.

Public education can play an important role in making people more aware of their responsibility for their own health. Children in all cultures are socialized to perform a myriad of self-preserving tasks, like brushing teeth or bathing, that are taken for granted as part of responsible human behavior. This basic competence can be expanded. School children can be taught the principles of treating simple illnesses, along with the basic warning signals of serious illness, and common-sense precautions about self-medication. The components of a healthy way of life, not just the ingredients of a balanced diet, can be part of every curriculum.

Self-care learning need not end with graduation; people should continue to have access to new information and motivation throughout their lives. The popularity of the women's book, *Our Bodies, Ourselves,* which has sold 2 million copies and been translated into thirteen languages, and of *Where There is No Doctor,* a self-care book originally written for Mexican peasants and now translated into four languages with more than 220,000 copies in print, indicates that people are hungry for this kind of information. Community-based self-care education programs already exist in many communities in the United States, following the pioneering example of Georgetown University's Course for Activated Patients in Washington, D.C., which teaches people to identify common health problems and treat everyday illnesses. Public self-care education can be beneficial. A study of both inner-city and suburban participants in the Georgetown program showed that they used professional care more appropriately and had lower laboratory and drug costs than a control group.[31]

The ultimate success of these health education and motivation programs may rest on the involvement of community organizations, such as churches and service clubs that exert influence over their constituents, but that have rarely played a role in health promotion. Heart disease, for example, is one of the main killers of men in clubs like the Lions or Kiwanis. These organizations, which often raise money for the treatment of illnesses, may want to turn some of their attention to educating their members about the prevention of illnesses. Much of the success of the cardiovascular disease prevention programs in California and Finland can be traced to just such involvement of community groups in changing unhealthy life-styles.

For their part, health care professionals must dare to relinquish some of the privileges and status of professionalism, and reconsider how they can best influence the health of their patients. In the future, the most important role of doctors may be as teachers, not as healers (after all, the word "doctor" comes from the Latin *docere*, "to teach"). Their biggest challenge may be to prolong a patient's life through new regimes of diet and exercise, rather than waiting to rely on expensive and often futile medical procedures. The medical profession's predilection for technology can be channeled into the development of new self-care technologies, such as a pocket apparatus to test for anemia, or simple flow charts that guide patients through a series of questions and answers to help them evaluate whether they should seek professional care.

Health care professionals can help their patients understand that doctors and nurses do not have magical curative powers to alleviate every ache and pain. They can remind themselves and their patients of Hippocrates's dictum that nothing is more natural than for the human body to heal itself, and that this process can take place without the aid of a physician. One of the most important things a doctor can accomplish is to help patients become active allies of the medical care system.

Finally, the medical community can join with philosophers and theologians to help people come to terms with illness and death. Medical discoveries that prolong human life hold out an implicit promise of universal good health and potential immortality. In the quest for the perfect diet or the correct exercise program, it is easily forgotten that most people experience symptoms of illness every month, that being sick is part of living, and that death is inevitable. Neither self-care nor preventive health measures can relieve people of the burdens of illness and death. Self-care is merely a way to gain some control over this process and to manage, not overcome, disease.

Changing unhealthy personal habits and helping people improve their competence to deal with simple illnesses are two activities that could have a broad and immediate impact on the human condition. Yet self-help programs can suffer many of the same problems encountered by any organized social effort. In the drug and alcohol fields, some organizations that began with the excitement and promise of helping people gain greater control over their lives have ended up as bureaucracies that foster dependency, or, worse yet, as cults. Working closely with neighbors of a different caste or race to clean up the village water supply in a developing country or to break a smoking habit in an industrial nation raises all sorts of interpersonal problems. Furthermore, even the most sensible self-care and preventive measures must compete with pressures to adopt a "modern" (unhealthy) life-style. It is difficult to practice even the most self-interested behavior, like breast-feeding, or bed rest because of a cold, in communities that scoff at such traditions.

Despite these problems, the growing interest in preventive medicine and self-care is an encouraging sign that individuals and communities want to begin to exert greater control over their own health. As they do so, the rewards will be better health and better health care for all.

7

Filling the Family Planning Gap

More than half of the world's couples do not have the opportunity to control their childbearing decisions. They do not have adequate information about the health implications of ill-timed childbearing; few receive feedback on the impact of their fertility decisions on their community; many do not have access to modern family planning methods; and few are actively encouraged to use them when they are available. The development of modern contraceptive technology has far exceeded humanity's ability to distribute it and to motivate couples to use it. People's inability to gain control over their fertility often undermines their struggle to gain some control over other aspects of their lives.[1]

In the United States, the young—both married and single —face particularly difficult barriers in their efforts to obtain information about contraceptives and to protect themselves from unwanted pregnancy. Racial minorities—the most disadvantaged groups in society—have the highest rates of unplanned pregnancies. In other parts of the world, no more than one out of ten couples in Africa and one out of five in the Middle East and on the Indian subcontinent use contraception.[2]

The implications for population growth of this gap in family planning services are becoming ever more apparent. As the eighties began, the world's population stood at 4.4 billion and was growing at 1.8 percent per year. At this pace, world population will double by the year 2025. Many demographers believe that the number of people on the globe will eventually reach 12 billion, a level that could overwhelm both the earth's biological systems and humanity's social systems.

An Individual Choice

While population concerns are global in scope, both the human suffering that rapid population growth causes and the childbearing decisions that lead to large families occur at the individual level. Thus, efforts to slow population growth must begin with each couple. Family planning really epitomizes a local solution to a global problem.

By looking at some successful family planning efforts, it is possible to assess how couples can effectively take control of their childbearing. In 1979, the initial report of the World Fertility Survey, covering fifteen developing nations and four developed countries, showed that about half the women of reproductive age who were interviewed said that they wanted no more children. This conviction has been put into practice by many of them. In the last decade, the use of birth control pills, intrauterine devices, and male and female sterilization— the three most effective means of contraception—rose markedly in both rich and poor countries. In Australia, England, Japan, and the United States, two-thirds of all married women now regularly use contraception. This proportion represents virtually all the women who are not already pregnant, interested in becoming pregnant, or unable to have children.[3]

As a result, a dramatic and prolonged fall in birth rates has occurred in the last decade in countries representing more than one-third of the world's population. The fall has been most dramatic in certain developing nations, notably China, Indonesia, and Colombia. But birth rates in industrial countries are also declining. The nations of Central and Eastern Europe, North America, and Scandinavia now have birth rates near replacement level, and some are even experiencing a slight drop in population size.[4]

This success is due in part to the availability of modern contraceptive technology, which enables couples to make rational plans regarding childbearing and to stick with them, rather than making hasty decisions in moments of passion. The development of simple and safe surgical sterilization techniques has meant that nearly one-third of all married couples of reproductive age in the United States now use this permanent family planning method. The convenience and reliability of birth control pills has led more than one-third of the couples in the United States and over half of those in Great Britain to choose this type of contraception. Use of the diaphragm, often considered an inconvenient method, is increasing in the United States because it gives women a sense of control over their bodies; backed up by legal abortion, this barrier method is one of the safest means of family planning. The liberalization of abortion laws in countries with about two-thirds of the world's population has also given women more control over childbearing. The availability of free contraceptives under national health service programs or public family planning programs and their uniform low cost throughout most of the industrial world means that most individuals can afford birth control if they can gain access to it and are encouraged to use it.[5]

Couples are choosing to use effective family planning methods and to have fewer children for a variety of reasons. The cost of raising a child, now more than $134,000 in the United States, is obviously one factor. In addition, the growing number of women who have an education or a job see options for themselves beyond the traditional role of mother and housekeeper. As the standard of living improves in some Third World countries, more children are surviving infancy, therefore it is no longer necessary to have a large family to ensure that one or two children will live to be adults.

But the decision to have a child is not the simple result of mixing a little education with a dash of affluence and a pinch of modern contraception. It is a highly complex process, subject to both personal impulses and social pressures. Where once the message from friends and relatives was in favor of large families, in a number of countries there are now significant pressures to have only one or two children.

Peer pressure may be the critical factor in motivating people to take control of their fertility and solve their own population problems. For example, a generation ago, when women in North America sat around in college dormitories or on their coffee breaks they often discussed marriage and children. Today in those same settings they are much more likely to be discussing careers or other means of personal fulfillment. Their expectations for themselves are different. Their attitudes toward childbearing have changed, in part because they are influenced by their friends whose attitudes are also changing. Studies of this mutually reinforcing dynamic by Sharon Houseknecht of Ohio State University indicate that, at least for those women who decide not to have any children at all, social approval from important peers is the key link between career orientation and childlessness.[6] Only further research will clarify the role of peer pressure in the decisions of more and more couples to have only one or two children, but it is clear that no one decides in a social vacuum whether or not to have a child. The success of efforts to slow population growth may ultimately depend on society's ability to consciously articulate peer pressure to influence childbearing decisions.

A Community Responsibility

Childbearing is a social act. It has an immediate impact on the community and its ramifications are felt for generations. The people down the block whose neighborhood is getting more crowded, the elected officials who must plan future schools, and the farmer who must grow more food are all affected by a new birth. Everyone feels the consequences of rapid population growth, so everyone has a stake in family planning decisions. As economic and environmental conditions deteriorate this stake will increase. While the primary rights and responsibilities of having a baby are personal, there is no way to separate the act of childbearing from its social context.

Until recently, official family planning programs ignored the community's stake in childbearing decisions. The role that friends and neighbors can play in influencing those decisions was disregarded. Now there is growing evidence that through the involvement of local communities in distributing contraceptives and motivating their users, family planning programs can reach those who are not yet effectively planning their families.

For example, the Chinese launched a community-based family planning program in the early seventies. By 1976, the International Planned Parenthood Federation estimated that 37 percent of married couples in China practiced contraception. Moreover, reports from several large cities indicate that more than half of all urban Chinese couples of reproductive age use contraception. According to official Chinese statistics, the population was growing at only 1.2 percent per year in 1978 and growth was expected to slow to a remarkably low 0.5 percent per year by 1985.[7]

This achievement is due to the fact that population growth

has become the concern of the whole community. Networks of small birth planning groups exist in factories, neighborhoods, and villages. Five to ten couples meet once or twice a year to plan among themselves the number of births for their group for that year. Schooled by their experiences in local planning for agricultural and industrial production, income distribution, and social welfare, these groups fully understand the cost to the community of excessive childbearing. They set local population growth goals that are coordinated with targets set by regional and national agencies. Once the number of births for a factory or a neighborhood group has been established, the birth planning group members allocate the births among themselves. Pi-chao Chen, one of America's foremost experts on Chinese family planning, reports that couples are given priority in the following order: first are the newly married, who are free to have their first child without delay; second are couples with only one child; and third are couples whose youngest child is nearest five years of age. It is not known whether this method of group planning, which was apparently first developed in Shanghai in the early seventies, has been fully adopted in rural areas, but travelers in China report the existence of birth planning groups in the most remote provinces.[8]

Chinese family planning officials attribute the success of birth planning groups to patient persuasion by peers. Formal family planning incentives do, however, exist. In 1979, the government promulgated a birth planning law designed to encourage one-child families. This law included child care subsidies, and housing and educational benefits for families who "stopped at one." But even the manner in which this law was developed is indicative of the Chinese commitment to community involvement in family planning. "In accordance with the Chinese practice of 'mass line,' " writes Pi-chao Chen, "the government circulated a preliminary draft of the law among all the basic level units throughout the country. 'The masses' were asked to debate the specific provisions proposed in the draft and to channel upward their comments and reactions. Taking into account the feedback from below, the government revised the original draft and formally promulgated the birth planning law."[9]

The birth planning groups serve to inculcate certain social values: that each couple is entitled to, but should have no more than, one or two children, irrespective of personal preference, social status, or income; that couples should not marry until the combined ages of the bride and groom equal at least 50 years; and that women should be freed from the burden of endless childbearing so that they may become men's equals. Birth planning groups also facilitate the distribution of contraceptive services, avoiding the inefficiencies of government bureaucracy that have encumbered efforts in other countries. Every office or workplace has one person in charge of carrying on family planning education and distributing pills and condoms. In addition, one of the residents of each of the courtyards around which houses are clustered is responsible for birth planning matters.

The Chinese family planning system was designed to distribute contraceptives and encourage their use on a massive scale in a country with meager incomes and too few trained personnel. Such a decentralized program can only work when the efforts of local groups are backed up by government support. The country's highest administrative body, the State Council, similar to the Cabinet in many countries, has a Birth Planning Office. A pension system in urban areas and guarantees of basic necessities for childless couples in the countryside have reduced dependence on children for old-age security. The national health service, paid for by the central government and local communities, provides all contraceptive services—including sterilization and abortion on demand—at no charge. But the key to the effectiveness of the Chinese program has been the state's ability to make the small family a national goal and to involve community groups in implementing that goal. Only recently have those directing family planning programs in other countries recognized the benefits of pursuing such a course.

One such nation is Indonesia, where, in the early seventies, a new sense of the urgency of slowing population growth emerged. From the office of the president on down, public officials realized that family planning could not be left solely within the purview of the minister of health. Population pressure came to be viewed as a problem affecting general community development, and thoughtful Indonesians recognized that birth control efforts should be made a community rather than a central government undertaking.

Originally the Indonesian government tried to establish a clinic-based family planning program. When the program failed to increase contraceptive use significantly, the National Family Planning Coordinating Board (BKKBN) redesigned its programs to reflect the social structures and decision-making patterns of Indonesian village life. For centuries in Bali, family heads have met every month to make decisions affecting the whole village. In Java, the elected or traditional headman of each hamlet commands both respect and obedience. So the BKKBN turned to these authority figures—the headman and the decision-making bodies—for help in recruiting contraceptive users and in selling villagers on the idea of small families.[10]

In response to the complaints of village women about traveling long distances to obtain contraceptive supplies, the Indonesian government has established some 27,000 village pill and condom depots in Java and Bali. In some villages, women needing supplies simply pick them up at the distributor's home. Increasingly, however, women assemble at monthly meetings of the local Mothers' Club, or *Apsari*, to buy their contraceptive supplies at nominal fees and to discuss their health problems. Extensive charts and lists are kept and displayed, a subtle way to build support for family planning because every villager knows who is not using contraception.

In most villages, the *Apsari* meet in the headman's house under his watchful eyes. When a woman drops out of the group or stops using contraception, the headman is likely to call her in for a talk and members of the *Apsari* may visit her to discuss the matter.

"At first this strategy stopped just short of coercion, and stirred resentment," notes Richard Critchfield, the only Western journalist regularly reporting from Third World villages. "But then the Javanese discovered what every anthropologist, but almost no development economist knows; the most potent force in every village is neither government fist nor religious belief; rather it is fear of the neighbour's censure or 'what will people say?' So family planning was plugged into existing social networks and local leaders were given responsibility for spreading it. The traditional Javanese hierarchical structure and the social pressure it brings to bear did the rest."[11]

The focus of the *Apsari* groups has widened to include other community self-help activities that introduce women to alternative and supplementary roles to motherhood. Several groups have started cooperative rice-savings banks, thus developing food reserves for their villages. Others have created small savings and loan operations, lending money to start community gardens or stores or to support special projects like the repair of irrigation works. In each case women are solving local problems while enhancing their own roles in the community.

Community-based family planning in Indonesia is working. Data from the World Fertility Survey indicate that 37 percent of all women practice contraception. The figures suggest that birth rates have dropped faster in Java and Bali in recent years than in any other developing country, with the possible exception of China. Moreover, a whole range of fertility-related activities, such as the registration of births and marriages and the distribution of contraceptives, are now carried out at the community level. Some villages have even raised the local legal age of marriage. Such local initiative is encouraging. For as Haryono Suyono of the BKKBN points out, "The long term success of family planning in Indonesia hinges on the ability of the government to transfer to the individual and the community the same sense of urgency that now exists at higher levels of government rather than simply imposing a family planning program on an otherwise uncommitted public."[12]

In South Korea, Mothers' Clubs handle contraceptive distribution and motivation. Originally, the Korean family planning
program depended on field workers who were individually responsible for reaching over 2,000 couples each, in as many as
fifty to sixty villages—an overwhelming caseload. To rectify
this situation, the Planned Parenthood Federation of Korea
reorganized and expanded its family planning services through
clubs modeled on traditional village organizations. Today,
women meet in the homes of their elected club leaders to
receive their monthly supply of pills or condoms, and to discuss
the value of small families and child-spacing. Despite the opposition of some bureaucrats who would like to see the women
focus almost exclusively on birth control, the Mothers' Clubs
emphasize overall village development. Nearly three-quarters
of them have established credit unions. Others have initiated
reforestation projects, developed new rice lands, bought livestock herds, and opened grocery stores.[13]

While the family planning programs in most developing
countries are more effective in urban than in rural areas, the
Korean program is almost equally effective in both, and the
Mothers' Clubs deserve much of the credit. According to
Worldwatch Institute researcher Kathleen Newland, "The
Mothers' Clubs network—with more than 27,000 clubs and
over 750,000 members—constitutes a double attack on population growth by providing its members with contraceptive services and advice on the one hand and status, income, and
psychological support on the other."[14]

Family planning programs that engage the users of contraceptive services in educating and motivating themselves have
also proved successful with adolescents. Traditional, adult-ori-
ented birth control programs, which treat people as passive
clients of a government service, have generally failed to reach
teenagers. As a result, less than one-third of sexually active
never-married American teenagers regularly use some method
of birth control, while a survey in Kenya among sexually active 15- to 19-year-old women showed that seven out of ten

could not name one contraceptive method.[15]

In response to such failures, new peer-oriented programs have sprung up. "Grapevine," Britain's community sex education project for adolescents, trains young volunteers to work with people their own age in coffee bars, in pubs, and on the streets. Teen counselors distribute condoms to those requesting them and refer interested young women to teen clinics where they can get medical advice and contraceptives. This program, which started in London, has expanded to other British towns and has been replicated in West Germany.[16]

Because of a shockingly high rate of venereal disease among students, "rap sessions" on adolescents' problems led by trained volunteer peer counselors have been organized during school hours in many New York City high schools. In 1974, Woodson High School in Washington, D.C., established one of the first school-based contraceptive clinics in the United States. Peer counseling goes on during class hours, and students can have physical examinations and obtain contraceptives from the clinic in the school nurse's office at the end of the day. The results of such initiatives have been encouraging. In the first three years that school-based family planning clinics were open in two Saint Paul, Minnesota, high schools, adolescent pregnancies declined by 40 percent.[17]

One of the few teen-oriented family planning efforts in the Third World is CORA, which opened its doors in 1978 in the middle-class Napoles section of Mexico City. Young people meet there for group discussions about sexuality and sexual responsibility. They can also see a doctor who regularly visits the center, and obtain contraceptives if needed. Of equal importance, the teens are trained to give talks in their schools and to act as information resources for their friends, so that street-corner sex education, still the way that most children learn the facts of life, is more accurate and informative.[18]

There is every reason to believe that these programs will prove successful because they are rooted in adolescent society. Projects like CORA include a variety of social activities—

language courses, a Boy Scout troop, and some group therapy —and thus appeal to a broad range of adolescent interests and problems. They create a mini-community that can shape adolescent values, including those about sexual responsibility. And since this community is run by young people, it can open doors to the teenage psyche for which no adult has the key. "We go out and talk to kids till we're blue in the face," observes Claire Parker of Planned Parenthood in Rochester, New York, "but when the peer counselors go out, they get through."[19]

The importance of these programs transcends their impact on teen fertility. By helping adolescents deal with their sexuality, peer-oriented family planning efforts enable young people to sense the power of determining their own destinies. And by accomplishing this in a collective manner they teach teens a firsthand lesson in mutual aid.

Any attempt to influence a couple's childbearing decisions clearly poses a threat to freedom of choice. In 1976, for example, India had a short-lived policy of forced sterilization of men with several children. A number of other nations have offered financial incentives to couples to have small families and have begun to penalize people who have large families. If the populations of some countries double and triple within a generation, as current trends indicate they will, a Malthusian hysteria about food shortages or runaway inflation might tempt governments to resort to even more coercive measures to slow population growth, with little concern for the individual.

Peer pressure to have a small family does indeed constrain individual options. Yet as the world becomes more crowded, it will be necessary to make society's interest in family size more explicit. The individual's right to choose how many children he or she has must be balanced against the community's right to protect itself from growing too large too quickly. From the standpoint of human freedom it is far better for people to impose their own limits on fertility with help from their friends and neighbors than to have the government do it for them.

Helping Couples Plan Their Families

Although the potential exists for individual couples to consciously control their fertility and for communities to put the
brakes on population growth, they cannot do it alone. Ensuring
that the 350 million couples who do not now practice family
planning have access to birth control will require concerted
public support.

Even the most extensive community-based family planning
programs need government funding. The Indonesian government, for example, spent eleven dollars for each contraceptive
acceptor in 1973/74. Overall, this amounted to about 40 percent of its annual health budget. Without international assistance, it would be impossible for many countries to maintain
this level of support without diverting resources from other
important development programs. Since 1970, international
financial resources available for family planning have more
than doubled. But even this dramatic expansion of funds has
not kept up with demand. According to the United Nations
Fund for Population Activities, at least one billion dollars a
year will be needed to increase the worldwide supply of contraceptives, subsidize their distribution, and perfect new contraceptive technologies.[20]

For their part, national governments can help create a legal
and social atmosphere in which individual family planning has
a chance to work. Laws relating to abortion, sterilization, and
contraceptives can be liberalized and updated. Sex education
can become an integral part of school curriculums and can be
encouraged in informal educational settings. Governments can
change laws and influence social customs, such as the age of
marriage or the role of women in society, that affect fertility.
Innovative development strategies that encourage fertility decline need support, as do broad-based efforts to fully educate
the public about the consequences of rapid population growth.

Central governments can set the tone for a national discussion of future population growth. The Chinese have done this quite effectively. Peking supplies villages with information about the relationship between population size and resources and about the problems China will face if population continues to increase. Then villagers make their childbearing decisions knowing full well the consequences if they decide to persist in having large families. Establishing the small family as a national goal, and creating the framework in which that goal can be debated and affirmed, can lend added legitimacy to family planning.

Finally, in structuring their official family planning programs, governments must never forget that the people who use the services should control the programs. Just as there is no best contraceptive for all couples, there will be no single way to meet family planning needs. Only if each community designs its own family planning activities so that they are sensitive to local value systems and life-styles will individual childbearing decisions be responsive to long-range community interests.

8

Helping People Help Themselves

Individuals and communities cannot create local solutions to global problems in isolation. Public policies in support of self-help efforts are often necessary to overcome some of the human and institutional obstacles that stand in the path of people helping themselves. Just as an oyster needs to have a grain of sand inserted in it before it can create a pearl, a community often needs outside assistance in order to help itself.[1]

In the minds of many people, there is an inherent contradiction in government support for self-help activities. According to this view, local endeavors can only succeed if they are free from government intervention. This distinction, while ideologically neat, is not appropriate for the complex issues facing society over the next few decades. There can be no clean division between public and private roles in problem solving.

Much has been written in recent years about the merits of solving problems from the bottom up—starting with local efforts—rather than solving problems from the top down—beginning with action by the government. But concentrating authority and responsibility at the local level is no more a sure prescription for success than is concentrating them at the national or international level. Many current issues require a new public policy framework in which the ultimate authority for defining the broad outlines of policy is centralized and the responsibility for actual problem solving is decentralized.

Coping with rising energy prices, for example, requires that governments, in consultation with citizens, establish national energy-consumption goals and mobilize public support for those goals. This task calls for a wide range of centralized resources—technical experts capable of dealing with production and distribution questions, economists able to assess the impact of various energy alternatives on the economy, and diplomats who can smooth the political waters to ensure a steady flow of oil from the Middle East. But since higher energy prices have their greatest impact at the local level, it is there that energy issues must ultimately be resolved. Decentralized energy conservation and solar energy programs—like those in Davis, California, and Portland, Oregon—can enable citizens to gain control over the energy issues that most affect their lives and help them to develop efficient, sustainable sources of power that are appropriately matched with local needs. Such a two-pronged approach to issues can combine centralized and decentralized resources to solve problems effectively.

From the Top Down

In the past, there has been little connection between narrowly focused individual and community self-help activities and broader efforts to effect political and economic change. Self-help initiatives by the poor have been struggles for survival rather than attempts to reform society. Individualistic fads—like EST and transcendental meditation—have left their marks on people's psyches but not on their social institutions. Community self-help efforts—such as Youngstown, Ohio's attempt to keep a steel mill running under local ownership—have been frustrated because they were not part of a broader movement to restructure the economy to make such activities viable. To overcome such limitations of self-help efforts, links need to be established between local activities and initiatives to solve problems at the national and international level.

Governments can help forge these links by providing citizens with information about the relationship between their problems and broader issues—establishing the connection between local population growth and national food shortages, for example. Moreover, official pronouncements, speeches by government leaders, and the general tone of public policies can create an aura of legitimacy for local problem solving and send a message to citizens that they are expected to become more involved in public life. Charismatic leaders can personify the values inherent in self-help activities and lead a public debate on the role of self-help efforts in modern society.

The structure of national governments can be a hindrance to self-help efforts, since the very size of most bureaucracies often makes person-to-person interaction difficult and limits government ability to provide local groups with financial and technical assistance. Thus at every level of government—local, state, national, and international—there is a need to create a parallel structure of small agencies and special offices that are of the appropriate scale and scope to foster particular self-help activities. The U.S. government, for example, already has an Urban Homesteading Division within the Department of Housing and Urban Development, and an urban gardening program within the Department of Agriculture. Individuals and communities can turn to these offices and get assistance tailored to their particular needs.

Governments may want to go one step further and create a high-level independent office that can coordinate government support for a whole range of local activities, making certain, for instance, that self-help housing projects include solar energy applications and community gardens wherever possible. This office could also act as an advocate for community groups and monitor the work of government bureaucracies to ensure that their programs do not smother local initiatives. Such an entity —located in the president's or prime minister's office, or established as a semi-autonomous body—could provide broad leadership, both inside and outside government, for self-help efforts.

Local activities also need the investment of public resources to augment the investment of private resources by individuals and communities. This will be a delicate process. Supporting a food co-op is much more complex than funding the building of a dam, because human beings, not bricks and mortar, are the core of the project. Not enough money at the right time can doom worthwhile efforts, and too much money inappropriately administered can transform vital indigenous programs into second-rate bureaucratic endeavors.

Governments are accustomed to ladling out money in large portions, but most self-help programs need only a dollop of funds. In huge bureaucracies like the World Bank, the paperwork for a small grant or loan can cost more than the actual dollar value of the assistance. For this reason, governments need to form special funding mechanisms that can provide the $10,000 or $15,000 in loans, grants, or loan guarantees needed to get a local project off the ground.

A self-help fund, supported by a fixed portion of each government's agency's budget and run jointly by people from the bureaucracy and local communities, could be established to provide the seed money for projects like housing cooperatives or worker-owned factories. Taking money from each department's budget in this way would symbolize government commitment to reducing public dependence on the state. Direct funding would keep the bureaucratic overhead to a minimum and enable national governments to support innovative activities at the local level. Using public funds to support self-help ventures can have a substantial payoff. The Office of Neighborhood Self-Help Development in the Department of Housing and Urban Development estimates that for every million dollars it invests in self-help projects, $16 million is contributed from local resources. Few government programs can boast of such a return on the public's money.[2]

Public support for self-help activities calls not only for a restructuring of government, but also for a fundamental change in the way that the state initiates and manages its programs. To reestablish personal contact between the government and the governed, bureaucrats need to get out of their offices and into local communities. A dialogue at the local level between bureaucrats and citizens is essential. Such a dialogue would permit people to explain their most pressing problems, to outline what they want to do about these issues, and to describe the actions they expect government to take. Self-help solutions imposed from above will not reflect people's perceptions of their own needs and abilities and are therefore likely to fail.

Self-help community development programs in Africa, Asia, and Latin America in the fifties and the U.S. War on Poverty in the sixties failed in part for precisely this reason. Projects were parachuted into communities where no one had asked for them and where they had little connection with local political and economic realities. The programs made the mistake of either aligning themselves with local elites, who were often part of the problem, or bypassing the community power structure completely, engendering political opposition and undermining their chances for success. The decentralization of problem solving came with such suddenness that unprepared local groups were overwhelmed. It is little wonder that many programs failed and that the resultant backlash led to further centralization of government programs.[3]

To avoid these mistakes, national government support for self-help programs can focus on efforts that respond to needs identified by the community. Decentralization can be a measured process that evolves as communities decide they are ready for it. Projects must be controlled by the people they are meant to serve, and programs must be founded on local partnerships between the powerful and the powerless that are based on jointly defined goals. To establish this cooperation, governments must be willing to pressure disparate local groups to sit down together and discuss self-help activities.

Finally, support for self-help projects will require new criteria for measuring the success or failure of government endeavors. The shortcomings of quantitative indicators in assessing self-help programs need to be acknowledged. For example, there is no way to quantify the value of public participation in decision making, for the importance of people having greater control over their own lives is as much a philosophical and psychological issue as it is a practical one. Government programs frequently measure success entirely in practical terms by changes in macroeconomic indicators, like per capita income or the gross national product—standards that are wholly inappropriate for assessing self-help efforts. At the very least, new microeconomic indicators are needed, ones that can measure things like the value of a food-buying club in an urban ghetto or of a neighborhood energy-auditing program. Moreover, there is a need for a dependency index that measures the success of government programs by the degree to which projects increase citizen self-reliance.

Initially, self-help programs will be experiments; support for them will necessarily be a learning process for the governments and citizens involved. An uncommonly high degree of failure is inevitable and should be accepted as the price society pays for innovative, humanistic projects. The ultimate success of government support for self-help efforts will not be measured by the amount of money disbursed or the number of people who participate, but by the long-term viability of the social processes funded—processes through which individuals and communities not only solve problems, but also gain skills and confidence that will benefit them long after specific government projects have ended.

From the Bottom Up

Local self-help activities have all too often been episodic and disorganized. Practical initiatives like gardening or housing renovation have been one-dimensional. Organized mutual aid groups have made little effort to relate their activities to those of other self-help organizations. Fragmented self-help efforts are like the pieces of a mosaic that need to be assembled into a coherent pattern, so that attempts to overcome alcoholism, for example, can complement community mental health campaigns.

Innovative local leadership can act as a catalyst to bring disparate self-help activities together, building partnerships between community groups that have skills and groups that have needs. A resourceful leader can broker the various interests in a community to ensure that the success of self-help efforts by one group is not achieved at the expense of another. Being a leader of self-help activities demands more, however, than the mere definition of a path that others must follow. Leadership requires an understanding of group dynamics and skill in building a consensus. It requires someone who can deal with the confusion, the ambiguity, and the contradictions of participatory decision making. Self-help activities depend on leaders committed to their communities and to the proposition that people are the best judges of their own interests. Above all, they require people who can lead a group by helping the group to lead itself.

To ensure continuity in local problem solving, self-help efforts need an organizational framework. The most appropri-

ate structure for self-help activities are local social networks—
the web of friends and acquaintances that surrounds each person. The most intimate social networks are made up of people
who encounter each other informally on a daily basis. As ur-
banologist Jane Jacobs describes them, they grow out of "people stopping by at a bar for a beer, getting advice from the
grocer. . . . Most of it is ostensibly utterly trivial, but the sum
is not trivial at all. This sum of such casual, public contact at
the local level . . . is a feeling for the public identity of a people,
a web of public respect and trust, and a resource in time of
personal and neighborhood need."[4]

Informal networks often coalesce into formal ones, ranging
from prayer meetings and social clubs to recreational associations and ladies-aid societies. Over half the adults living in
Western Europe belong to at least one such group. In some
countries, like the Netherlands and Denmark, the proportion
is as high as 75 to 80 percent. French historian Alexis de
Tocqueville's observation a century and a half ago, that
"Americans of all ages, all conditions and all dispositions form
associations" still holds true today. According to recent estimates there are now nearly six million private voluntary associations in the United States.[5]

These groups provide an ideal setting for self-help activities.
Most cultures have a tradition of mutual aid or cooperative
projects rooted in community relationships—such as barn rais-
ings, fraternal burial societies, and group savings organizations.
National programs that have worked through social networks
and local organizations to solve community problems have a
good record. A Cornell University study of rural development
programs in sixteen Asian countries found that the most successful were linked with participatory local organizations. A
similar study of eleven Asian, African, and Latin American
countries by Development Alternatives, a consulting firm,
showed a clear connection between the success of rural development projects and the involvement of small farmers through
their local organizations.[6]

Social networks are a useful vehicle for organized self-help activities because the mutual understanding, shared values, and common perspective that they foster enable people to work together effectively. The loose-knit structure and the small size of these networks permit them to be flexible and to develop solutions that are unique to particular settings. People are directly accountable for their actions when they work in small groups, a powerful incentive for individuals to act responsibly. The equitable nature of the internal structure of many small groups permits a fair distribution of the benefits of self-help activities. And because people control community groups, adjustments can easily be made if self-help efforts are not working. Since small groups and organizations are on a human scale, efforts to solve problems through them can generate solutions that are sensitive to human needs.

Linking Local and National Self-help Efforts

The state needs some formal relationship with community networks to establish which activities and responsibilities should be left at the local level and which ones should be centralized, to link national support for self-help activities with local efforts, and to orchestrate community involvement in self-help projects. The United States has much to learn in this respect from other countries. In Italy and France, these functions are often performed by neighborhood organizations that are affiliated with national political parties, thus community activities are part of a grand social strategy. In Central Java, Indonesia, the connection between the government and the community is embodied in the village headmen. Many of these headmen are former military officers, all are lifelong residents of their villages; they can be depended upon to orchestrate local self-help activities within the constraints of national policy. In China, the link between Peking and the commune is membership in the Communist party. Party members, who are also members of production brigades or birth planning groups, are responsible for ensuring continuity between local activities and the broader goals of society as defined by the party.

In the United States, the same kind of liaison between the federal government and self-help networks could be established through the creation of neighborhood self-help councils. The most important function of these councils would be to involve formal and informal community groups in redefining the social contract, thereby establishing anew the rights and duties of both citizens and their government. The councils could organize the voluntary associations that make up social networks into forums for local participation in the formulation of public policy. In the mid-seventies, Sweden attempted just such an effort, when the government called upon the public to help create a national energy policy. Unions, adult education centers, and political parties organized courses on energy issues in which citizens analyzed energy alternatives and made formal recommendations to the government. More than 70,000 people took part, the equivalent, on an American scale, of nearly 2,000,000 citizens being involved in shaping national policy.[7]

In addition, the councils could help coordinate the direct involvement of formal and informal networks in a variety of self-help activities. They could work with businesses to train energy auditors, with schools to give courses in housing rehabilitation, with libraries to organize a tool lending system, and with service groups to turn vacant lots into community gardens. They could help citizens focus on new areas of concern for their communities, such as displacement of low-income residents or a rise in adolescent pregnancies. The councils could be instrumental in forming new self-help groups around these issues—a housing rehabilitation cooperative or a teen counseling service. By bringing people together to solve problems, councils could form new social networks that complement existing ones, strengthening the community's social fabric.

Neighborhood councils would also work to bring together the federal government and citizens in new private-public part-

nerships. These partnerships could be modeled on Neighborhood Housing Services, a project to combat housing abandonment and displacement, in which the U.S. government provides the financial and technical resources and local
communities provide the housing stock and the political will
to deal with shelter problems. Similar innovative programs
combining national and local resources are needed to weatherize old buildings or to develop food and energy cooperatives.
These partnerships would be based on the principle that community organizations should match any government funding
for their projects with several times the equivalent in local
funds or donated labor.

Despite their informal connection with the state, self-help
councils would not be neighborhood governments. No community would be required to have a self-help council; governments
would encourage their formation, but the main impetus would
come from the local level. A clear delineation of the councils'
responsibilities would be made so that they do not become just
extensions of the public bureaucracy, as that would mean they
had lost their natural roots in the community and thus their
effectiveness.

Each community could organize its councils in its own manner. Some would want to elect council members directly, others might want them to be appointed by prominent neighborhood organizations. They would make no pretense of being
representative democratic institutions. Rather, they would be
participatory organizations, open to all those who care to be
involved in finding solutions to community problems.

The Obstacles to Self-help

Public support for self-help efforts must take into account
the difficulties inherent in translating local initiatives into
broader social policies. As Witold Rybczynski of McGill University has observed, "Small is not always beautiful, local is not
always better."[8] Economic reality is a constraint on even the

most well-intentioned self-help efforts. The success of self-help activities often depends on people working without pay. Beyond a certain point, however, reliance on donated labor can be just another means of exploitation, and is bad economics as well. If the only way to keep a worker-owned factory solvent is for employees to work overtime at low wages, it may be better for them to find other means of employment.

Self-help efforts can also have unforeseen consequences that offset the advantages of people doing more for themselves. For example, the growing use of wood-burning stoves in Aspen and Vail, Colorado, has led to a serious air pollution problem. Before supporting self-help efforts, governments must be sure to assess both the pros and cons of such endeavors.[9]

Even where support is justified, there are many impediments to self-help activities. Some obstacles are rooted in the nature of human beings, some in the character of human organizations, and some in the power structure of society.

Basic human insecurity leads citizens to sit in isolation in their suburban homes; fear of the consequences of change encourages the poor to passively live out their existences in the slums of Third World cities. Many people are reluctant to become actively involved in the world around them. They cling to class, ethnic, and racial distinctions as a safe definition of themselves and others. Dependence on institutions and experts comes easily, for it creates psychological security by leaving responsibility to someone else. Self-interested behavior in the pursuit of short-term security can be a compelling force that often drives people to work against their own and their fellow human beings' long-term interests.

Insecurity is deeply rooted in people's psyches. Extreme poverty robs individuals of their hope, and political oppression gives them legitimate reason to fear taking risks. These conditions breed apathy that will not easily be overcome. To break out of this state of powerlessness, people need support for taking charge of the particular issues—like housing or energy—that directly affect their lives. Public policies that sustain such activities can create a secure atmosphere in which individuals feel free to become involved, to take risks, and to work with others.

There are other practical human constraints on self-help efforts. Helping oneself is time-consuming—modern homesteaders can expect to spend as much as one and one-half hours per square foot of floor space in building their homes. Many people may want to allocate their time in other ways. Moreover, some people will always be more willing than others to take the time and effort to participate in self-help activities.

Efforts to involve social organizations in self-help activities for the first time will encounter similar problems. Local groups can be parochial and insular, hidebound by tradition. Voluntary service organizations, for example, often concern themselves with the alleviation of immediate human suffering, like caring for the blind or sheltering the homeless. They rarely engage in self-help efforts to overcome the social and economic causes of problems—the nutritional deficiencies that lead to childhood blindness or the obstacles to homeownership by the poor.

This myopia is partly the result of self-imposed prohibitions on even faintly political activities. In a world where problem solving is becoming increasingly political, this posture is naively self-defeating. By creating a legitimate role for local organizations in the solution of economic and political problems, public policies can encourage community groups to remove their political blinders and to actively exert their influence.

The nature of society—its culture, traditions, and social norms—will also help determine the boundaries of self-help activities. For example, the caste system in India creates deep cleavages in communities and makes broad-based self-help efforts difficult. In contrast, the success of local self-help activities in China and Indonesia is due in part to the close-knit social structure that exists at the community level. In both these countries, strong family ties and cultural uniformity bind villages together in a way not found in many other societies, making it easier for people to work together. While self-help activities are not culture specific, they cannot be expected to bridge the generation-old divisions that separate many ethnic or racial groups. In many American neighborhoods, for example, community gardens are primarily intended to grow vegetables, not heal old wounds. Initially, self-help projects will be most successful when they are confined to cohesive, relatively homogeneous groups.

Powerful institutions—the state bureaucracies, the corporations, and the professions—have an inherent antagonism toward self-help efforts because such activities pose a challenge to the existing order. For example, the American Medical Association has generally resisted self-care medicine, partly because any dilution of doctors' responsibilities is a threat to their power. Many governments may pay only lip service to self-help programs or actually oppose them because they realize their democratizing potential. Certainly, authoritarian political systems are less fertile breeding grounds for self-help activities than democratic systems. Yet even the most undemocratic local or national government faces a dilemma today because its legitimacy, like that of all governments, is partly based on the ability to solve problems. The growing difficulties encountered by centralized efforts to cope with current issues, coupled with the success of decentralized activities, has led a number of governments to grudgingly acknowledge the viability of self-help projects.

The opportunity will always exist for the establishment to manipulate self-help programs, and to use them to absolve those in power of responsibility for problems that are manifestly beyond individual and community control. The inherent political potential of self-help efforts is the best insurance against this prospect. As individuals and communities solve local problems they gain power. Moreover, citizens learn political skills—how to organize a meeting, how to build a coalition, and how to exert their influence. They can use this power and these talents to assert their legitimate role in the solution of society's problems and to force governments to act in the public interest.

The historical landscape is dotted with the ruins of grand social experiments based on naive and simplistic assumptions about innate human goodness. People are considerably more capable and responsible than paternalistic stereotypes would suggest, but they are also less virtuous and wise than many would like to assume. Similarly, their community organizations can be vibrant, resourceful groups, or moribund, impotent institutions.

Establishing the limits to self-help activities is a political exercise of fundamental importance. Individuals and communities will differ markedly in what they want and in what they can and should do for themselves. One group's idea of self-reliance could easily be another group's concept of dependence. A self-help program in the inner city will require a different type of government support than one in a small town and will have different consequences. The economic needs, the social backgrounds, and the philosophies of the people involved are all relative. In order to accommodate these differences, self-help programs need to grow out of a political process in which local groups can shape the programs meant to help them. Designing a public policy framework in support of self-help activities can help people help themselves by incorporating the advantages of centralization with the benefits of decentralization.

9

Empowering Ourselves

In the next few decades, humanity can begin to solve some of its most pressing problems through local self-help efforts. The most important benefit of these activities, however, will not be more housing or better nutrition, but the values articulated in the process of meeting basic human needs. These values will outlive society's deeds. They will shape people's sense of their own abilities, determine their future success in solving problems, and ultimately enable individuals and communities to gain greater control over their lives.

Individuals have historically relied on their communities for survival. Because of this dependence, communities have traditionally been the source of people's values. But as governments, corporations, and professional elites have gradually assumed

responsibility for the provision of human needs, they have also
begun to shape human values, fostering dependency, helplessness, and powerlessness.

Obviously, most people have neither the time nor the resources to do everything for themselves. But, in the name of
convenience, dependency has been stood on its head and cele-
brated as a virtue. There is a pervasive misconception that it
is one of the benefits of affluence, a sign of status, to no longer
concern oneself with mundane activities like gardening or
breast-feeding.

These misguided values are no longer viable. They grew out
of a centralized system of fulfilling human needs that current
economic and environmental conditions have rendered obso-
lete. More important, the psychology of dependency has no
place in a humanistic world. It is based on depersonalized
relationships between people and institutions, not on human
interaction within communities. Moreover, dependency leads
to a power imbalance in society. As individuals and communities give up control over the issues that affect their lives, political power is concentrated more firmly in the hands of the state
and corporations.

New values of self-reliance and individual and collective
competence are needed to replace the ethic of dependency and
helplessness. These humanistic values assert the dignity and
worth of individuals and their social institutions, and affirm the
capacity of people and their communities to cope with a complex world. They reflect the growing significance of individual
and community problem solving in today's world.

These values can be formed through self-help activities.
Planting a garden or rehabilitating a house is a learning process.
Individuals define for themselves the extent of their dependence and their potential for self-reliance. They come to understand how their own values about energy use, for example,
must change in response to dwindling energy resources. And
through working with others to solve problems, people create
new social norms—such as energy conservation—that are rein-
forced through human interaction.

The creation of new values through local-level self-help efforts can pose problems. Community value systems can be restrictive and stultifying. New ideas develop slowly in small towns and close-knit neighborhoods, and even the most positive changes can be stymied by tradition. Individual rights are often not respected. Indeed, racial segregation in the United States was the result of such closed-minded values. Similarly, any conscious effort to rapidly change values threatens to be manipulative and to ride roughshod over human sensibilities. Throughout history, one of the redeeming virtues of community-based value systems has been that they have changed slowly, in an organic fashion that has permitted people to adjust to them gradually.

Community-based value systems must protect individual rights, while being flexible enough to reflect emerging social concerns. In order to safeguard human freedom and to ensure that value changes are sensitive to local concerns, it is necessary to involve as many people as possible in the definition of new values. School segregation would not have been the norm in the United States, for example, if blacks had been able to vote in school-board elections. Moreover, to ensure that local values do not contravene the broader goals of a just and sustainable society, communities and national governments need to work out a framework of basic human rights that a central authority is empowered to enforce.

The shaping of self-reliant human values plants seeds of change, for the process of local problem solving and value formulation empowers people. English philosopher John Stuart Mill argued more than a hundred years ago that even if bureaucrats were more efficient at solving problems it was better for citizens to do things for themselves because such efforts expanded their abilities. Similarly, Alexis de Tocqueville felt that the greatest value of the jury system was not what it did for the accused, but what it did for the jurors themselves, by involving them in the direct exercise of political and legal power. Today, psychologists and educators call this the helper-therapy principle. Alcoholics and mental patients who help treat others having the same illness tend to have a higher recovery rate than those who are only recipients of treatment. Children with reading problems show dramatic improvement in their reading levels if they become teachers in their own right, helping younger pupils learn to read. "Whoever wants to know a thing has no way of doing so except by coming into contact with it," observed Mao Tse-Tung. "If you want knowledge, you must take part in changing reality."[1]

Each individual's efforts to solve his or her problems and to create new values can become part of a broader process of social change. As S. F. Jencks points out with regard to self-care, "If participatory care gains wide acceptance, it will be accompanied by a revolution in the social structure of medicine. The rigid hierarchical structure in which all knowledge and planning flow downwards from the physician cannot survive the transition to participatory forms of care."[2]

The political ramifications of current self-help efforts are only beginning to be felt. Chilean sociologist Ignatio Balbontin's studies of employees in worker-managed factories indicate that they are more active in politics and community life than employees in traditionally-organized businesses.[3] Similarly, the women in the Mothers' Clubs of Indonesia and South Korea have not been content to narrowly focus their energies on family planning. They realize that the welfare of their villages rests on the resolution of a whole range of economic and environmental issues and their efforts to solve these problems include exerting political pressure on their governments. The various community self-help movements in Western Europe and the United States have led to experiments with neighborhood government as a way for people to exercise greater control over social services. Italy now has neighborhood governments in more than 130 cities, more than a dozen American cities have neighborhood councils or advisory commissions, and New York City alone has more than 10,000 block clubs that have some say over life in their communities.

It is too soon to assess the full social and political impact of self-help activities, but such efforts can lead to more equitable political systems. Governments reflect the power structure of their societies. In the Third World, as long as the church, the landed aristocracy, and the military have formal responsibility for solving problems, they will continue to hold political power. In North America and Western Europe, if bureaucrats, businessmen, and professionals continue to play an ever larger role in public life, the democratic voice of the average citizen will grow fainter. However, if individuals and communities can do more to help themselves, and if their role in meeting basic human needs can be institutionalized in local social networks, then the power that accompanies the ability to solve problems will be spread among a broad segment of the population. Thus, the challenge of building democratic, participatory societies is not simply a question of revamping electoral systems or reorganizing bureaucracies; citizens must also be involved in numerous enterprises ranging from the improvement of health care to the management of industry.

Self-help efforts have long been considered props of the status quo. They have the inherent potential, however, to change the system. The self-help process, as Eugene Meehan points out in his study, *In Partnership with People,* is "a metaphorical time bomb in the culture. Its ultimate repercussions are beyond calculation, but its justification is found in the essential commitment to allowing men to make their own destiny as best they can."[4]

Historically, violent political revolutions have been based on people's efforts to control their own destinies. Today, there is the opportunity for a quiet revolution, one based on people helping themselves. Citizens can create a parallel system for solving problems at the local level that is an alternative to big bureaucracies and corporations staffed by technocrats. This process of community capacity building and citizen empowerment can open up economic and social life and lay the foundation for a society that is truly responsive to the needs and feelings of all its citizens.

Notes

1. Introduction

1. "Capitalism: Is It Working?," *Time,* April 21, 1980.
2. Federal Trade Commission, *Economic Report on Trends in Aggregate Concentration* (Washington, D.C.: forthcoming).
3. "Opening the Tax Battle," *Time,* July 7, 1980; Policy Planning and Program Review Department, *Global Estimates for Meeting Basic Needs: Background Paper* (Washington, D.C.: World Bank, 1977); John G. Sommer, *Beyond Charity* (Washington, D.C.: Overseas Development Council, 1977).
4. Ivan Illich, *Toward a History of Needs* (New York: Pantheon Books, 1978).
5. *Public Opinion,* October/November 1979.
6. Philip M. Mbithi and Rasmus Rasmusson, *Self-Reliance in Kenya* (Uppsala, Sweden: Scandinavian Institute of African Studies, 1977).

2. Worker Participation

1. Maccoby quoted in *Alternatives in the World of Work* (Washington, D.C.: Committee on Alternative Work Patterns, and the National Center for Productivity and the Quality of Working Life, Winter 1976); George Morris, "A Management-Union Approach to Improving Quality of Work Life," presented to the Society of Automotive Engineers, Detroit, March 2, 1977.

2. Bureau of Labor Statistics, "International Comparisons of Manufacturing Productivity and Labor Costs, Preliminary Measures for 1979," press release, U.S. Department of Labor, Washington, D.C., May 22, 1980; U.S. Congress, Joint Economic Committee, *Soviet Economic Problems and Prospects,* Committee Print, August 8, 1977; Denison quoted in Jerry Flint, "Inflation Slows Productivity," *New York Times,* May 27, 1978.
3. Survey Research Center, "The 1977 Quality of Employment Survey," University of Michigan, Institute for Social Research, Ann Arbor, Mich., 1978; "Australia: Survey on Absenteeism," *Social and Labour Bulletin,* June 1978; M. Holubenko, "The Soviet Working Class: Discontent and Opposition," *Critique,* No. 4, 1975.
4. Melvin Kranzberg and Joseph Gies, *By the Sweat of Thy Brow* (New York: G. P. Putnam's Sons, 1975); Matt Witt, "Dangerous Substances and the U.S. Worker: Current Practice and Viewpoints," *International Labour Review,* March/April 1979; "Why Workers Want to Flee U.S.S.R.," *U.S. News & World Report,* May 29, 1978.
5. Taylor quoted in David Jenkins, *Job Power* (New York: Penguin Books, 1974).
6. Weir quoted in Nat Hentoff, "Working, Schmoozing, and Paying Dues," *Social Policy,* November/December 1978.
7. Material on the Bolivar experiment drawn from Daniel Zwerdling, *Workplace Democracy: A Guide to Workplace Ownership, Participation and Self-Management in the United States and Europe* (New York: Harper & Row, 1980); Michael Maccoby, "Changing Work," *Working Papers for a New Society,* Summer 1975; Margaret Molinari Duckles, Robert Duckles, and Michael Maccoby, "The Process of Change at Bolivar," *Journal of Applied Behavior Science,* July/August/September 1977; and Kathy Terzi, Harvard University Project on Technology, Work and Character, Washington, D.C., private communication, May 25, 1978.
8. Swedish Ministry of Labor, "Towards Democracy at the Workplace," Stockholm, January 1977; Andrew Martin, "From Joint Consultation to Joint Decision Making: the Redistribution of Workplace Power in Sweden," *Current Sweden,* June 1976; "What's Happening," *Sweden Now,* Vol. 10, No. 1, 1976.
9. American Center for the Quality of Work Life, *Industrial Democracy in Europe* (Washington, D.C.: 1978); Michael Rubenstein, "Volkswagen, Works Councils Given Joint Control over Work Measurement in New Contract for West German Plants," *World of Work Report,* May 1979.
10. Material on worker participation in Japan drawn from Benjamin Roberts, Hideaki Okamoto, and George Lodge, *Continuity and Change in the Industrial Relations Systems in Western Europe, North America, and Japan* (New York: Trilateral Commission, May 1978); Joji Arai, speech presented to the Industrial Engineering Shipbuilding Conference, Atlanta, Georgia, February 23, 1978; Robert E. Cole, *Japanese Blue Collar: The Changing Tradition* (Berkeley: University of California, 1971); Robert E. Cole, *Work Mobility and Participation: A Comparative Study of American and Japanese Industry* (Berkeley: University of California, 1979); Mitz Noda, "Business Management in Japan," *Technology Review,* June/July 1979.
11. Information on the Yugoslav experience drawn from Howard Wachtel, "Participatory Planning and Management: An Issue Paper," unpublished, American University, Washington, D.C., March 1978; G. David Garson, *On Democratic Administration and Socialist Self-Management: A Comparative Survey Emphasizing the Yugoslav Experience* (Beverly Hills, Calif.: Sage, 1974); and Zwerdling, *Workplace Democracy.*
12. Rick Levine, "Industry's Gamble: Giving Workers a Say," *The Record* (Bergen, N.J.), February 10, 1977; "Hot UAW Issue: 'Quality of Work Life,'" *Business Week,* September 17, 1979.
13. James Furlong, *Labor in the Boardroom* (Princeton, N.J.: Dow Jones Books, 1977); American Center for Quality of Work Life, *Industrial Democracy in Europe; Die Zeit* report discussed in Alfred Diamant, "Democratizing the Work Place: The Myth and Reality of *Mitbestimmung* in the Federal Republic of Germany," presented to Annual Meeting of the American Political

Science Association, Chicago, September 2–5, 1976.
14. Alfred Thimm, "Decision-Making at Volkswagen," *Columbia Journal of World Business,* Spring 1976; Robert Ball, "The Hard Hats in Europe's Boardrooms," *Fortune,* June 1976.
15. Donahue quoted in Zwerdling, *Workplace Demoracy.*
16. Karl Frieden, *Workplace Democracy and Productivity* (Washington, D.C.: National Center for Economic Alternatives, 1980).
17. Survey Research Center, "Employee Ownership," University of Michigan, Institute for Social Research, Ann Arbor, Mich., September 1977; U.S. Senate, Select Committee on Small Business, *The Role of the Federal Government and Employee Ownership of Business,* Committee Print, revised March 1979; Ann Crittenden, "Italy's Red-led Co-ops Prosper," *New York Times,* June 18, 1978; Robert Oakeshott, *The Case for Workers' Co-ops* (London: Routledge & Kegan Paul, 1978).
18. Jeremy Rifkin and Randy Barber, *The North Will Rise Again* (Boston: Beacon Press, 1978); John Curtis, Employee Stock Ownership Council, Los Angeles, private communication, October 31, 1978.
19. Zwerdling, *Workplace Democracy.*
20. U.S. Senate, *The Role of the Federal Government.*
21. Daniel Zwerdling, "Employee Ownership: How Well Is It Working?," *Working Papers,* May/June 1979.
22. Martin Carnoy and Henry Levin, "Workers' Triumph," *Working Papers for a New Society,* Winter 1976; Martin Leighton, "The Workers' Triumph," *Sunday Times Magazine* (London), June 4, 1978; Oakeshott, *The Case for Workers' Co-ops.*
23. Bruce Stokes, "Democracy in Chile: At Work in the Factory," *Washington Post,* October 22, 1978; Juan Espinosa and Andrew Zimbalist, *Economic Democracy* (New York: Academic Press, 1978); the material in this section is also based on the author's personal observations in Santiago, Chile, August 1978.
24. Suresh Srivastua et al., *Job Satisfaction and Productivity* (Springfield, Va.: National Technical Information Center, 1975); Frieden, *Workplace Democracy and Productivity.*
25. Roberts, Okamoto, and Lodge, *Continuity and Change.*
26. Paul Bernstein, "Worker-Owned Plywood Firms Steadily Outperform Industry," *World of Work Report,* May 1977; Frieden, *Workplace Democracy and Productivity.*
27. Survey Research Center, "Employee Ownership"; John R. Cable and Felix R. FitzRoy, "Productive Efficiency, Incentives and Employee Participation: Some Preliminary Results for West Germany," *Kyklos,* Vol. 33, 1980.
28. Senator Robert C. Byrd et al., "If Chrysler Workers Were Chrysler Stockholders," Letter to the Editor, *New York Times,* October 24, 1979.
29. Special Task Force to the Secretary of Health, Education, and Welfare, *Work in America* (Cambridge, Mass.: MIT Press, 1973).
30. Zwerdling, "Employee Ownership."
31. Agnelli quoted in *Industrial Democracy in Europe.*
32. Bureau of National Affairs, "Basic Patterns in Union Contracts," 9th ed., Washington, D.C., May 1979.
33. The German Marshall Fund of the U.S., "The West German Humanization of Work Program," unpublished, Washington, D.C., undated.
34. Jeremy Rifkin, *Own Your Own Job* (New York: Bantam Books, 1977); Zwerdling, "Employee Ownership".

3. The Consumer Energy Resource

1. Lilienthal quoted in Harold Faber, "Hydro-Electricity: Small Can Be Beautiful, as Well as Profitable," *New York Times,* September 23, 1979.
2. Denis Hayes, Worldwatch Paper 4, *Energy: The Case for Conservation* (Washington, D.C.: Worldwatch Institute, January 1976); Office of Conservation, "Conservation Facts for Speech Writers," U.S. Department of Energy, Washington, D.C., February 1980.

146:   Notes *(pp. 43–51)*

3. Office of Technology Assessment, *Residential Energy Conservation, Vol. 1* (Washington, D.C.: Congress of the United States, July 1979); "Energy Conservation: Results and Prospects," *OECD Observer,* November 1979.
4. Socolow quoted in Daniel Yergin, "Conservation: The Key Energy Source," in Robert Stobaugh and Daniel Yergin, *Energy Future* (New York: Random House, 1979).
5. Ibid.; Barbara and Alan Massam, "Poorly Insulated Buildings in UK called a 'National Scandal,' " *World Environment Report,* March 13, 1978.
6. Stobaugh and Yergin, *Energy Future;* Mary Rawitscher and Jean Mayer, "Energy, Food, and the Consumer," *Technology Review,* August/September 1979.
7. Richard J. Cattani, " 'Materialism' Called Drag on Fuel Conservation Drive," *Christian Science Monitor,* November 14, 1977; Office of Technology Assessment, *Residential Energy Conservation;* "Energy Conservation: Results and Prospects."
8. "Energy Conservation: Results and Prospects"; Lester R. Brown, Christopher Flavin, and Colin Norman, *Running on Empty: The Future of the Automobile in an Oil-Short World* (New York: W.W. Norton & Co., 1979).
9. Jerry Knight, " '80 Forecast: 50% Small Cars," *Washington Post,* July 19, 1979; Lew Pratsch, U.S. Department of Energy, private communication, May 13, 1980; Statistical Department, *Transit Fact Book,* 1977–78 Edition (Washington, D.C.: American Public Transit Association, 1978); Bicycle Manufacturers of America, private communication, August 29, 1979; Elizabeth Pond, "Will West Germans Use Their Bikes?," *Christian Science Monitor,* November 8, 1978; "Look Ma, No Pollution!," *EPA Journal,* October 1978.
10. Roger Sant, "The Least-Cost Strategy: Minimizing Consumer Energy Costs Through Competition," Mellon Institute, Arlington, Va., June 1979; Stobaugh and Yergin, *Energy Future;* Karl Frieden, *Workplace Democracy and Productivity* (Washington, D.C.: National Center for Economic Alternatives, 1980).
11. Philip F. Palmedo and Pamela Baldwin, "The Contribution of Renewable Resources and Energy Conservation as Alternatives to Imported Oil in Developing Countries," Energy/Development International, Port Jefferson, N.Y., 1980. The authors of this study acknowledge that because of the paucity of data from the Third World these estimates are necessarily rough.
12. Elizabeth Cecelski, Joy Dunkerley, and William Ramsay, *Household Energy and the Poor in the Third World* (Washington, D.C.: Resources for the Future, July 1979); Arjun Makhijani, *Energy Policy for the Rural Third World* (London: International Institute for Environment and Development, 1976).
13. Palmedo and Baldwin, "The Contribution of Renewable Resources."
14. Denis Hayes, Worldwatch Paper 11, *Energy: The Solar Prospect* (Washington, D.C.: Worldwatch Institute, March 1977).
15. Science Council of Canada, *Canada as a Conserver Society: Resource Uncertainties and the Need for New Technologies* (Ottawa: 1977); Thomas B. Johansson and Peter Steen, "Solar Sweden," *Ambio,* Vol. 7, No. 2, 1978; Peter Curliani, Solar Energy Industries Association, private communication, February 1980.
16. Hayes, *Energy: The Solar Prospect;* Roger N. Morse, "Solar Energy in Australia," *Ambio,* Vol. 6, No. 4, 1977; Abe Rabinovich, "More Than One in Ten Israelis Heat with Solar Energy Units," *World Environment Report,* March 24, 1980.
17. Denis Hayes, Solar Energy Research Institute, private communication, May 22, 1980; Harvey Wasserman, The Clamshell Alliance, private communication, July 13, 1977.
18. Material on Davis, Calif., is drawn from James Ridgeway, *Energy-Efficient Community Planning: A Guide to Saving Energy and Producing Power at the Local Level* (Emmaus, Pa.: J.G. Press, 1979); Robert Lindsey, "Town Learning to Live with Less Energy," *New York Times,* July 18, 1979; Melinda Beck, "Energy: Start Small," *Newsweek,* October 8, 1979.
19. Material on San Luis Valley, Colo., is drawn from Bill Kovarik, "San Luis: Most Solarized Community in the Nation," *AT Times,* January/February 1980; "San Luis Future Power: A Program to Enable a Community to Create Its Own Energy Future," Rocky Mountain Center on Environment, Denver, Colo., 1978.

20. Center for Renewable Resources, *Shining Examples: Model Projects Using Renewable Resources* (Washington, D.C.: 1980).
21. Bruce Stokes, "Society's Little Platoons: A Web of Respect and Trust," *The Baltimore Sun*, March 19, 1980.
22. Cecelski, Dunkerley, and Ramsay, *Household Energy*.
23. Erik Eckholm, Worldwatch Paper 26, *Planting for the Future: Forestry for Human Needs* (Washington, D.C.: Worldwatch Institute, February 1979).
24. Gasoline price increase in 1979 from National Foreign Assessment Center, "International Energy Statistical Review," National Technical Information Service, March 26, 1980; the cost per mile of running a car is the author's calculation based on figures in Office of Technology Assessment, "Automobile Transportation System," Vol. II, Technical Report," Congress of the United States, undated.
25. Projections of fleet average fuel economy from Richard Shackson, Mellon Institute, private communication, June 14, 1979; average distance driven by American automobiles from Motor Vehicle Manufacturers Association, *MVMA Motor Vehicle Facts & Figures, '78* (Detroit: undated); calculations by the author.
26. American home heating oil consumption figure from Richard Holt, U.S. Department of Energy, private communication, April 1, 1980; Office of Conservation, "Conservation Facts"; Assistant Secretary for Conservation and Solar Applications, *Tips for Energy Savers* (Washington, D.C.: U.S. Department of Energy, March 1978).
27. Palmedo and Baldwin, "The Contribution of Renewable Resources."
28. "Saving Costly Energy with People Power," *U.S. News & World Report*, April 7, 1980; Mark Cooper, "Energy Policy and Jobs," remarks to the AFL-CIO Conference on Energy and Jobs, Washington, D.C., May 5, 1980; E. Ariane van Buren, "Biogas Beyond China: First International Training Program for Developing Countries," *Ambio*, Vol. 9, No. 1.
29. David F. Salisbury, "Reducing High Energy Costs," *Christian Science Monitor*, March 3, 1980; "New Opportunities for Community-Based Energy Audit Programs: The Anacostia Experience," *Self-Reliance*, No. 20, undated.
30. "Canadian Energy Conservation Grants," *The Neighborhood Works*, November 9, 1979; James J. Kilpatrick, "Where Energy Conservation Works," *The Washington Star*, October 20, 1979; Diana Raines, California Energy Commission, private communication, June 11, 1980.
31. "We Are Running on a New Solar Strategy: Interview with Secretary Schlesinger," *Business Week*, October 9, 1978.
32. Denis Hayes, Worldwatch Paper 19, *The Solar Energy Timetable* (Washington, D.C.: Worldwatch Institute, April 1978); Rabinovich, "One in Ten Israelis Heat with Solar," Jered Beeby, San Diego County Government, private communication, June 11, 1980.
33. Marion Hemphill, energy advisor, city of Portland, private communication, August 13, 1979. Hemphill will provide copies of the Portland city legislation upon request. Dennis Bass, "Gushers in the City," *Environmental Action*, October 1979.
34. Mark Cherniak, "What One County is Doing to Earn Energy Freedom," *The Christian Science Monitor*, undated; "MA County Pioneers in Energy Planning," *The Energy Planning Report*, December 21, 1979.

4. A Roof Over One's Head

1. Department of Economic and Social Affairs, *Compendium of Housing Statistics, 1972–74* (New York: United Nations, June 1976); Department of Economic and Social Affairs, *World Housing Survey, 1974* (New York: United Nations, June 1976); Policy Planning and Program Review Department, *Global Estimates for Meeting Basic Needs: Background Paper* (Washington, D.C.: World Bank, August 1977).
2. William Young, National Home Builders Association, private communication, April 12, 1980; Office of Policy Development and Research, "Housing Costs in the United States and Other Industrialized Countries, 1970–1977," U.S. Department of Housing and Urban Development, Washington, D.C., September 1979;

"A Better Deal for Japan's Rabbits," *The Economist*, Feburary 2, 1980; World Bank, *Housing Sector Policy Paper* (Washington, D.C.: May 1975).

3. Rochelle L. Stanfield, "Caught in the Squeeze of the Rental Housing Market," *National Journal*, February 17, 1979; Roger Starr, "An End to Rental Housing?," *The Public Interest*, Fall 1979.

4. National Urban Coalition, *Neighborhood Transition Without Displacement: A Citizen's Handbook* (Washington, D.C.: 1979); Robert Reinhold, "Reversal of Middle-Class Tide Sets Poor Adrift in Some Cities," *New York Times*, February 18, 1979.

5. "Faulty Towers," *The Economist*, June 25, 1977.

6. Tomasz Sudra, "Can Architect and Planner Usefully Participate in the Housing Process? The Case of Ismailia," published privately, Somerville, Massachusetts, March 1979.

7. Bruce Stokes, "Tenant Management and Social Coehsion," *Washington Star*, April 21, 1980; "Britain's Council Housing," *The Economist*, September 8, 1979; Peter Osnos, "Another Way: Co-ops, Private Homes in the Soviet System," *New York Times*, November 23, 1976.

8. John F. C. Turner, British Architectural Association, private communication, August 14, 1977.

9. Larry Hays, *Building Supply News Magazine*, private communication, April 7, 1980.

10. Tom Black, Urban Land Institute, private communication, December 19, 1977.

11. Bryan Dyer, U.S. Department of Housing and Urban Development, private communication, December 12, 1979; Chris Orwick, "The Homesteaders," *New Society*, April 26, 1979.

12. William C. Grindley, "Owners-Builders: Survivors with a Future," in John F.C. Turner and Robert Fichter, eds., *Freedom to Build* (New York: Macmillan Co., 1972).

13. Turner, private communication.

14. Bruce Stokes, "Recycled Housing," *Environment*, January/February 1979.

15. Task Force on Governance, Citizen Participation, and Neighborhood Empowerment, *Case Study Appendix* (Washington, D.C.: National Commission on Neighborhoods, 1979); Gail Robinson, "When the Rich Return," *Environmental Action*, September 9, 1978.

16. Frances Potts, Banana Kelly Community Improvement Association, private communication, April 10, 1979.

17. Office of Policy Development and Research, "The National Tenant Management Demonstration: Status Report Through 1978," U.S. Department of Housing and Urban Development, Washington, D.C., 1978; Alan S. Oser, "The Problem of Managing Properties Seized by City," *New York Times*, March 16, 1979.

18. Islington resident quoted in Anne Power *Facts and Figures About the Holloway Tenant Co-operative* (London: North Islington Housing Rights Project, 1979); Anne Power, *Holloway Tenant Cooperative* (London: North Islington Housing Rights Project, 1977).

19. Urban Homesteading Assistance Board, "Third Annual Progress Report," New York, April 1977; Rural Housing Alliance, "Self-Help Housing Projects: 1978 Survey," Rural America, Washington, D.C., August 1979; conversion estimates based on a 1978 study by Multi-Family Housing Services, Oxon Hill, Md., for the Webster House Tenant Association, Washington, D.C.

20. Sudra, "The Case of Ismailia."

21. Bruce Hannon et al., "Energy and Labor in the Construction Sector," University of Illinois, Urbana-Champaign, Ill., September 1977; Bruce Hannon and Richard Stein, private communication, June 9, 1978; Richard G. Stein, *Architecture and Energy* (Garden City, N.Y.: Anchor Press/Doubleday, 1977).

22. Rural Housing Alliance, "Self-Help Housing Projects."

23. Roger Mann, "Solving the Housing Problem," *Africa Report*, May/June 1978.

24. Richard Martin, "Housing Options, Lusaka, Zambia," *Ekistics*, August 1977.

25. Timothy Cullen, World Bank, private communication, December 1979.

26. Cost estimates by the author based on a World Bank self-help housing project in

Indonesia; Harold B. Dunkerley, "Serviced Sites and Squatter Upgrading Projects: The World Bank Experience," *The Urban Edge*, December 1979; Sally Cameron, "Local Participation in Bank-Supported Urban Development Projects," World Bank, Washington, D.C., March 1978.

27. Robert Hanley, "Homesteading, Urban Style, Yields Oak Floors and More," *New York Times*, December 23, 1979.
28. The material on Baltimore is based on the author's visit to the city on May 12, 1978.
29. Urban Systems Research and Engineering, Inc., *Urban Homesteading Catalogue, Vol. 2* (Washington, D.C.: Prepared for the U. S. Department of Housing and Urban Development, August 1977); Bernard Cohen, "Rehabilitating Sweat Equity-Part 1," *City Limits*, February 1980.
30. Robert Hale, "In the Netherlands," *Ekistics*, March/April 1979; National Urban Coalition, *Neighborhood Transition*.
31. Roger S. Ahlbrandt, Jr., and Paul C. Brophy, "Neighborhood Housing Services: A Unique Formula Proves Itself in Turning Around Declining Neighborhoods," *Journal of Housing*, No. 1, 1976; Rochelle L. Stanfield, "The Neighborhoods—Getting a Piece of the Urban Policy Pie," *National Journal*, April 22, 1978.
32. John F. C. Turner, *Housing by People* (London: Marion Boyars, 1976).

5. Small Is Bountiful

1. Comptroller General of the U.S., "Food Price Inflation in the United States and Other Countries," U.S. General Accounting Office, Washington, D.C., December 1979; European food prices based on figures published in *EEC Monthly Journal of Statistics Bulletin*, April 1978; J. Dawson Ahalt, "Meeting Tomorrow's World Food Needs," paper presented at the International Mineral and Chemical Corporation's 14th Latin American Food Production Conference, San José, Costa Rica, December 6, 1978.
2. Yi-Fu Tuan, "The City: Its Distance From Nature," *Geographical Review*, January 1978.
3. Gardens for All, "Summary of the 1979 National Gardening Survey Conducted by the Gallup Organization for Gardens for All," National Association for Gardening, Burlington, Vt., 1980.
4. This estimate of Third World gardening is based on several national studies, including Florentino S. Solon et al., "Vitamin A Deficiency in the Philippines: A Study of Xerophthalmia in Cebu," *American Journal of Clinical Nutrition*, February 1978; and Pan American Health Organization, "The National Food and Nutrition Survey of Guyana," Washington, D.C., 1976. Peltzer quoted in Anne Stoler, "Garden Use and Household Consumption Patterns in a Javanese Village," Department of Anthropology, Columbia University, July 1975.
5. Stoler, "Garden Use."
6. Pete Riley, *Economic Growth* (London: Friends of the Earth, 1979).
7. B. H. Thompson, Gardens for All, private communication, undated; Jamie Jobb, *The Complete Book of Community Gardening* (New York: William Morrow & Co., 1979).
8. Gardens for All, "Gardening in America 1978," National Association for Gardening, Burlington, Vt., 1979.
9. Material on Chicago, Los Angeles, and New York gardening programs from Bruce Stokes, "The Urban Garden: A Growing Trend," *Sierra*, July/August 1978.
10. The best work on private agriculture in the Soviet Union is Karl-Eugen Wädekin, *The Private Sector in Soviet Agriculture* (Berkeley: University of California Press, 1973). See also: Ian H. Hill, "The 'Private Plot' in Soviet Agriculture," *Journal of Peasant Studies*, July 1975; John W. De Pauw, "The Private Sector in Soviet Agriculture," *Slavic Review*, March 1969; T. Khadonov, "Regulating the Development of the Private Household Plot," *Problems of Economics*, January 1978.
11. U.S. home vegetable production author's calculations based on various yields using Gardens for All, "Summary of the 1979 National Gardening Survey," and U.S. Department of Agriculture, *Agricultural Statistics 1978* (Washington, D.C.: Government Printing Office, 1978). Russian production from Anton Malish, U.S.

Department of Agriculture, private communication, April 9, 1980.
12. Author's calculations based on U.S. Department of Agriculture, *Agriculture Statistics 1978;* Judy Loomis, Gardens for All, private communication, June 12, 1980.
13. Bruce Butterfield et al., "Teeming Tenth-Acre," *Gardens for All News,* Winter 1979/80; Miranda Smith, Institute for Local Self-Reliance, and Texas Agricultural Experiment Station staff members, private communications, August 1977.
14. Kenneth R. Walker, *Planning in Chinese Agriculture* (London: Frank Cass & Co., 1965); Agriculture and Rural Development Department, Nutrition Division, "Colombia: Appraisal of an Integrated Nutrition Improvement Project," World Bank, Washington, D.C., August 1977.
15. Gardens for All, "Summary of the 1979 National Gardening Survey"; Louise Cook, "Gardening: $3 to $5 an Hour Is Your Return," *Washington Post,* May 13, 1978; Rudolf Klein, "Britain's New Urban Peasants," *Washington Post,* September 4, 1977.
16. Wädekin, *The Private Sector;* Walker, *Planning in Chinese Agriculture.*
17. Stoler, "Garden Use."
18. David J. Morris and Gil Friend, "Energy, Agriculture, and Neighborhood Food Systems," Institute for Local Self-Reliance, Washington, D.C., 1975.
19. Lerza quoted in "Urban Food," *The Elements,* May 1978.
20. Colin Hines, "Crops and Shares," Friends of the Earth, London, 1976; Science Council of Canada, "Canadian Agriculture in the Year 2001: Scenarios for a Resource-Efficient Agriculture and an Eco-Agriculture," Macdonald Stewart Institute of Agriculture, October 1977.
21. Author's estimate based on U.S. Department of Housing and Urban Development, *National Survey of Abandonment* (Washington, D.C.: undated).
22. The 5 percent figure from The Trust for Public Land. For further information on neighborhood land trusts, contact The Trust for Public Land, based in Oakland, Calif., and Newark, N.J.
23. Karl Munson, U.S. Department of Agriculture, private communication, April 3, 1979.
24. Brezhnev quoted in "Facing Food Problems, Moscow is Encouraging Private-Plot Farmers," *New York Times,* July 10, 1977; *The Constitution of the People's Republic of China* (Peking: Foreign Language Press, 1978); Thomas Wiens, Mathtec, Inc., private communication, March 27, 1979.
25. Thomas J. Marchione, "Food and Nutrition in Self-Reliant National Development: The Impact on Child Nutrition of Jamaican Government Policy," *Medical Anthropology,* Winter 1977.
26. Community Renewal Team of Greater Hartford, "Hartford Food System, Inc.," Hartford, Conn., November 1978.
27. Campaigne Mondiale Contre la Faim, *Rapport au Gouvernement du Dahomey: L'Amélioration de la Nutrition par la Création des Jardins Familiaux* (Rome: Food and Agriculture Organization of the United Nations, 1973); Aminata Tal, "Co-Op Gardens Boost Status of Women in Rural Senegal," *Christian Science Monitor,* June 21, 1978.
28. Sri Setyati Harjadi, *Improvement of the Home Garden in the Context of the Family Nutrition Improvement Programme of the Government of Indonesia* (New York: UNICEF, 1977). Material in this section is also based on the author's visit to Gendeng, Central Java, March 1977.
29. Kevin Klose, "Brezhnev Demonstrates His Political Grip Is Still Strong," *Washington Post,* December 3, 1978; Roger Mann, "Tanzania's Collectives Reap Little Food, Much Hostility," *Washington Post,* February 7, 1977.
30. James Pines, Transcentury Fund, private communication, March 26, 1979; Lester Tepley, UNICEF, private communication, January 23, 1980; Paul Sommers, UNICEF consultant, private communication, December 20, 1979.

6. Taking Responsibility for Health

1. Erik P. Eckholm, *The Picture of Health: Environmental Sources of Disease* (New York: W. W. Norton & Co., 1977); M. Gregg Bloche, "China Discovers Health Perils Accompany Modernization," *Washington Post,* August 19, 1979; Public

Health Service, *Health-United States, 1978* (Washington, D.C.: U.S. Department of Health, Education and Welfare, 1978).

2. Carter quoted in Alan L. Otten, "Politics and People," *Wall Street Journal,* February 24, 1977.

3. Lowell S. Levin, "Self-Care: An International Perspective," *Social Policy,* September/October 1976; Public Health Service, *Health-United States 1978.*

4. Lowell S. Levin, Alfred H. Katz, and Erik Holst, *Self-Care* (New York: Prodist, 1976).

5. Eckholm, *Picture of Health;* Erik Eckholm and Kathleen Newland, Worldwatch Paper 10, *Health: The Family Planning Factor* (Washington, D.C.: Worldwatch Institute, January 1977); Latham quoted in Boyce Rensberger, "Drop in Breast Feeding Causes Health Problems in Poor Countries," *New York Times,* April 6, 1976.

6. Robert Gibson, U.S. Department of Health and Human Services; private communication; Brian Abel-Smith and Alan Maynard, *The Organization, Financing and Cost of Health Care in the European Community* (Brussels: Commission of the European Communities, 1978); Fredrick Galladay, *Health Sector Policy Paper* (Washington, D.C.: World Bank, 1980).

7. Steven Jonas, "Rx for Health Care Delivery," *Environment,* March 1980; Thomas McKeown, *The Modern Rise of Population* (New York: Academic Press, 1976).

8. Victor Cohn, "Low-Fat, High-Fiber Diet Is Urged to Lessen Risk of Cancer," *Washington Post,* October 3, 1979; Eckholm, *Picture of Health;* Concern, Inc., "Overfed and Undernourished?," *Points of View: A Nutrition Report,* January 1979.

9. Ralph Paffenbarger, "Exercise and Its Role in the Prevention of Cardiovascular Disease," in *New Directions in Health* (Denver, Colo.: Gates Foundation, 1979); estimates of the number of joggers based on several national polls including a 1979 National Survey of spare-time activities by the Gallup Organization.

10. Eckholm, *Picture of Health;* Public Health Service, *Health-United States, 1978;* "Less Ash About," *The Economist,* September 1, 1979.

11. Public Health Service, *Health-United States, 1978;* Nedra B. Belloc and Lester Breslow, "Relationship of Physical Health Status and Health Practices," *Preventive Medicine,* Vol. 1, 1972; Paffenbarger, "Exercise and Its Role"; Eckholm, *Picture of Health.*

12. L. Paringer, A. Berk, and S. Mushkin, *Economic Cost of Illness, Fiscal Year 1975* (Washington, D.C.: Georgetown University, 1977); Judith Abramson, the Washington Hospital Center, private communication, June 21, 1980; American Cancer Society, *Cancer Facts and Figures, 1980* (New York: 1979).

13. Thomas J. Marchione, "Food and Nutrition in Self-Reliant National Development: The Impact on Child Nutrition of Jamaican Government Policy," *Medical Anthropology,* Winter 1977.

14. Eckholm and Newland, *Health: The Family Planning Factor.*

15. John W. Farquhar, "A Community-Based Approach to Preventing Stroke and Coronary Heart Disease," in *New Directions in Health.*

16. Iain Guest, "Preventing Heart Disease Through Community Action: The North Karelia Project," *Development Dialogue,* No. 1, 1978; Pekka Puska et al., "Changes in Coronary Risk Factors During Comprehensive Five-Year Community Programme to Control Cardiovascular Diseases (North Karelia Project)," *British Medical Journal,* November 10, 1979.

17. Eckholm, *Picture of Health;* Walter Sullivan, "China Takes Ambitious Steps to End a Deadly Fever," *New York Times,* September 17, 1979.

18. John L. McKnight, "Community Health in a Chicago Slum," *Development Dialogue,* No. 1, 1978.

19. Public Health Service, *Healthy People: The Surgeon General's Report on Health Promotion and Disease Prevention* (Washington, D.C.: U.S. Department of Health, Education and Welfare, 1979).

20. John Fry et al., "Self-Care: Its Place in the Total Health Care System," a report by an independent working party, Great Britain, 1973; Lois Pratt, "The Significance of the Family in Medication," *Journal of Comparative Family Studies,*

Spring 1973; Secretariat for Futures Studies, *Care in Society: A Project Presentation* (Stockholm: 1979); Poul A. Pederson, "Patientiers Selvbehandling Inden Henvendelse til Praktiserende Laege," *Ugeskrift For Laeger*, August 2, 1976; C. P. Elliott-Binns, "An Analysis of Lay Medicine," *Journal of the Royal College of General Practitioners*, April 1973.

21. "Groups Help Those Who Help Themselves," *Hastings Center Report*, October 1977.

22. George O., M.D., "Alcoholics Anonymous," *Journal of the American Medical Association*, September 27, 1976; Stuart Henry and David Robinson, "Understanding Alcoholics Anonymous: Results From a Survey in England and Wales," *The Lancet*, February 18, 1978.

23. Helen I. Marieskind, "Helping Oneself to Health," *Social Policy*, September/October 1976; Helen I. Marieskind and Barbara Ehrenreich, "Toward Socialist Medicine: The Women's Health Movement," *Social Policy*, September/October 1975.

24. Public Health Service, *Health-United States, 1978;* Frank Riessman, "The President's Commission on Mental Health: The Self-Help Prospect," *Social Policy*, May/June 1978.

25. James S. Gordon, "Final Report—Special Study on Alternative Mental Health Services," The President's Commission on Mental Health, Washington, D.C., February 1978; "Peer Mutual Aid Networks Reduce Rehospitalization of Mental Patients," *Self-Help Reporter*, March/April 1979.

26. L. Miller and J. Goldstein, "More Efficient Care of Diabetic Patients in a County-Hospital Setting," *New England Journal of Medicine*, June 29, 1972; P. H. Levins and A. F. Britten, "Supervised Patient-Management of Hemophilia," *Annals of International Medicine*, Vol. 78, 1973.

27. See, for example, Alfred O. Berg and James P. LoGerfo, "Potential Effect of Self-Care Algorithms on the Number of Physician Visits," *New England Journal of Medicine*, March 8, 1979.

28. Eric Ranawake, "WHO Seminar Encourages Ancient Healing Arts of Traditional Medicine," Depthnews Science Service, Manila, Philippines, April 29, 1977; Mahler quoted in Anil Agarwal, "Eye of Newt and Toe of Frog," *New Scientist*, November 2, 1978; M. Max Nebout, "Bilan de huit ans d'autotraitement des lepreux du Secteur No. 3 de Moundou," *Bulletin de la Société de Pathologie Exotique*, September/October 1974.

29. Howard S. Berliner, "Emerging Ideologies in Medicine," *Review of Radical Political Economics*, Spring 1977.

30. Owen quoted in David Robinson and Stuart Henry, *Self-Help and Health* (London: Martin Robertson, 1977); Carter quoted in Otten, "Politics and People."

31. Boston Women's Health Book Collective, *Our Bodies, Ourselves* (New York: Simon & Schuster, 1971); David Werner, *Where There Is No Doctor* (Palo Alto, Calif.: Hesperian Foundation, 1977); Keith W. Sehnert, "A Course for Activated Patients," *Social Policy*, November/December 1977.

7. Filling the Family Planning Gap

1. Bruce Stokes, Worldwatch Paper 12, *Filling the Family Planning Gap* (Washington, D.C.: Worldwatch Institute, May 1977).

2. William Burr Hunt II, "Adolescent Fertility—Risks and Consequences," *Population Reports*, July 1976; Alan Guttmacher Institute, "11 Million Teenagers," New York, 1976; International Planned Parenthood Federation, *IPPF Survey of Unmet Needs in Family Planning 1971–76* (London: December 1977).

3. Sir Maurice Kendall, "The World Fertility Survey: Current Status and Findings," *Population Reports*, July 1979; John C. Caldwell et al., "Australia: Knowledge, Attitudes, and Practice of Family Planning in Melbourne, 1971," *Studies in Family Planning*, March 1973; J. Peel and G. Carr, *Contraception and Family Design: A Study of Birth Planning in Contemporary Society* (New York: Churchill Livingstone, 1975); Population Problems Research Council, *Summary of Thir-*

teenth National Survey on Family Planning (Tokyo: Mainichi Newspapers, August 1975); Charles F. Westoff, "Trends in Contraceptive Practice," *Family Planning Perspectives,* March/April 1976.

4. Stokes, *Filling the Family Planning Gap;* United Nations, *Monthly Bulletin of Statistics,* New York, February 1980.

5. Westoff, "Trends in Contraceptive Practice"; Peel and Carr, *Contraception;* Lester R. Brown and Kathleen Newland, "Abortion Liberalization: A Worldwide Trend," Worldwatch Institute, Washington, D.C., February 1976.

6. Sharon K. Houseknecht, "Achieving Females and the Decision to Remain Child-less: A Missing Link," Ohio State University, Department of Sociology, Columbus, Ohio, 1978.

7. International Planned Parenthood Federation, *IPPF Survey of Unmet Needs;* Chen Muhua, "Birth Planning in China," *Family Planning Perspectives,* November/December 1979.

8. Pi-chao Chen, "On the Chinese Model of Group Planning of Birth," presented at the Conference on IEC Strategies: Their Role in Promoting Behavior Change in Family and Population Planning Programs, Honolulu, December 1–5, 1975. The material in this section is also drawn from Pi-chao Chen, *Population and Health Policy in the People's Republic of China* (Washington, D.C.: Smithsonian Institution, 1976); Carl Djerassi, "Some Observations on Current Fertility Control in China," *The China Quarterly,* January/March 1974; Penny Kane, "Family Planning in China," *World Medicine,* April 1976; and Pi-chao Chen with Anne Elizabeth Miller, "Lessons from the Chinese Experience: China's Planned Birth Program and Its Transferability," *Studies in Family Planning,* October 1975.

9. Pi-chao Chen, Wayne State University, private communication, August 10, 1979.

10. Selo Soemardjan, "Some Cultural Aspects of the Indonesian People," speech given to American embassy, Jakarta, Indonesia, December 4, 1969; Haryono Suyono et al., "Village Family Planning: The Indonesian Model," in *Village and Household Availability of Contraceptives: Southeast Asia,* Battelle, 1976; Laura Slobey, "The Village Family Planning Post Program," University of Hawaii, July 1976. Much of the material in this section is drawn from the author's observation of the BKKBN's program in Gendeng, Central Java, March 1977.

11. "Shame Is the Best Contraceptive," *The Economist,* November 25, 1978.

12. Haryono Suyono, "The Indonesian Family Planning Program," presented at Third International Population Conference of the World Population Society, Washington, D.C., December 6, 1976.

13. D. Lawrence Kincaid et al., *Mothers' Clubs and Family Planning in Rural Korea: The Case of Oryu Li* (Honolulu: University of Hawaii, undated); Fran Korten, Harvard University, private communication, April 8, 1977; Everett M. Rogers, et al., "Mothers' Clubs in the Diffusion of Family Planning Ideas in Korean Villages: An Illustration of Network Analysis," presented to American Association for the Advancement of Science, New York, January 26–31, 1975.

14. Kathleen Newland, Worldwatch Paper 16, *Women and Population Growth: Choice Beyond Childbearing* (Washington, D.C.: Worldwatch Institute, December 1977).

15. John F. Kantner and Melvin Zelnik, "Sexual and Contraceptive Experience of Young, Unmarried Women in the United States, 1976 and 1971," *Family Planning Perspectives,* March/April 1977; Hunt, "Adolescent Fertility."

16. Janet Evanson, *Grapevine* (London: Family Planning Association, December 1974); "Youth and Planned Parenthood," *International Planned Parenthood Federation Europe Regional Information Bulletin,* October 1976.

17. Charles and Bonnie Remsberg, "Do Teens Make Good Sex Counselors?", reprint by Planned Parenthood Federation of America of an article originally published in *Seventeen* (1975); Lyn Marmet, Planned Parenthood/Metropolitan Washington, private communication, February 18, 1977; Laura E. Edwards et al., "Adolescent Pregnancy Prevention Services in High School Clinics," *Family Planning Perspectives,* January/February 1980.

18. The material in this section is drawn from the author's observation of the CORA program in Mexico City, July 1978.
19. Parker quoted in Remsberg, "Do Teens Make Good Sex Counselors?."
20. Terence H. Hull, Valerie J. Hull, and Masri Singarimbun, *Indonesia's Family Planning Story: Success and Challenge* (Washington, D.C.: Population Reference Bureau, 1977); Thomas Reese, III, U.S. Agency for International Development, private communication, September 24, 1976; "Assistance for Population," Conference Paper IV, *Populi*, Vol. 6, No. 3, 1979.

8. Helping People Help Themselves

1. I am indebted to Eugene J. Meehan, author of *In Partnership With People* (Washington, D.C.: Inter-American Foundation, 1979) for the oyster analogy.
2. Joseph McNeeley, Office of Neighborhood Self-Help Development, U.S. Department of Housing and Urban Development, Washington, D.C., private communication, May 22, 1980.
3. Two useful overviews of the failures of past participatory community development efforts are David C. Korten, "Community Organization and Rural Development," The Asian Institute of Management, Manila, 1980; and Arthur J. Naparstek, "Policy Options for Neighborhood Empowerment," in Alan K. Campbell et al., *Urban Options* (Columbus, Ohio: Academy for Contemporary Problems, 1976).
4. Jane Jacobs, *The Death and Life of Great American Cities* (New York: Vintage, 1961).
5. "Adopting Yet Another Part of the American Way of Life?," *Euroforum,* November 23, 1979; Alexis de Tocqueville, *Democracy in America* (New York: The New American Library, 1956); "The Neighborhood Movement," *Self-Help Reporter,* undated.
6. Norman T. Uphoff and Milton J. Esman, *Local Organization for Rural Development: Analysis of Asian Experience* (Ithaca, N.Y.: Cornell University, Center for International Studies, undated); Development Alternatives, *Strategies for Small Farmer Development: An Empirical Study of Rural Development Projects* (Washington, D.C.: May 1975).
7. Alvin Toffler, *The Third Wave* (New York: William Morrow and Company, 1980).
8. Witold Rybczynski, *Paper Heroes: A Review of Appropriate Technology* (Garden City, N.Y.: Anchor Press/Doubleday, 1980).
9. Chris Perham, "Wood a Growing Energy Source," *EPA Journal,* April 1979.

9. Empowering Ourselves

1. Mill cited in Robert Nisbet, *Twilight of Authority* (New York: Oxford University Press, 1975); Alexis de Tocqueville, *Democracy in America* (New York: The New American Library, 1956); Alan Gartner, Mary Kohler, and Frank Riessman, *Children Teach Children: Learning By Teaching* (New York: Harper and Row, 1971); Mao quoted in Ruth V. Sidel, "Self-Help and Mutual Aid in the People's Republic of China," in Alfred H. Katz and Eugene I. Bender, eds., *The Strength In Us* (New York: New Viewpoints, 1976).
2. Jencks quoted in David Robinson and Stuart Henry, *Self-Help and Health* (London: Martin Robertson, 1977).
3. Ignatio Balbontin, Santiago, Chile, private communication, August 4, 1978.
4. Eugene J. Meehan, *In Partnership With People* (Arlington, Va.: Inter-American Foundation, 1979).

Index